Dark Psyc

&

The Art Of Reading

People

-2 in 1-

Signs A Toxic Person Is Manipulating
You And How To Handle It

By

Richard Martinez

Table of Contents

Dark Psychology Secrets

The Art of Reading People

1. Introduction

- Is someone making your life miserable?
- How do you recognize if someone is being manipulative, or persuasive?

There is a fine line between manipulation and persuasion. Much depends on the reason why the influencer is trying to talk you into doing something in the first place. Is a salesperson manipulating you to buy his wares, for his own profit? Or, is he persuading you because he genuinely believes in his product? Manipulation can come at you in many forms, from a colleague or a partner to someone you don't know.

We are often pressured into making social changes in our lives. There is nothing wrong with that if you are the one to make the decision for the sake of your own wellbeing. If though, someone makes you do something that you don't want to do, then it has become a form of bullying. It can be difficult to stand up to bullies, at any age. Though, if you want to be free of them, then you need to learn how to take back control.

Recognizing that you are a victim of coercion and manipulation, is important. If you can achieve this, then you are on your way to resolving the problem. By reading books such as this one, you will come to realize that you do have the power to change the situation.

Being a victim of manipulation is very intimidating. It makes you feel powerless because you don't have the confidence to stand up to the perpetrator. It is hurtful and emotionally draining, causing many to become socially reclusive. Learn how to turn away from people who might try to make you do things you don't want to do. Never become such a victim ever again.

This is a book that will show you the way to take yourself forward, with the tips provided. First, learn what a manipulative person is all about. Then learn about "yourself." Who "you" really are. How "you" can find the courage to take charge of "your" life. Know the manipulator, and know yourself.

How can a book sort out your life? Well, this one is going to show you how to identify manipulative individuals. They often have certain characteristics that stand out. it will guide you into becoming a stronger person. Once you are that person, you will be able to confront this issue and resolve it once and for all.

Learn how to break that cycle of unhappiness. With proven psychological processes to refer to, it will help you understand the science of manipulation. See how to break free from any manipulative person who happens to pass through your life. This book can turn your life around. Guiding you into making the right choices; in a sense, how to manipulate the manipulator. Don't keep putting it off. Every day that you delay, is another day of NOT being in control.

Once you accept that you are being manipulated, only then you can grasp the idea that you, "Yes, you," can do something about it. The concepts within this book will show you how to recognize the character traits of a manipulative person. Understanding what's happening to you is vital, so you can move on to the next stage of your life. Turn the pages and become a free person, under the influence of no-one but yourself.

2. The History of Persuasion

Behavioral Trait of Manipulation

Psychodynamics

Sigmund Freud followers may argue that we are all directed by our own hidden desires, which puts us at the mercy of being exploited. A manipulative person may use another person's personal desires to take control of them. Once captured, the manipulator will influence in such a way that their captive has limited self-control. Although Freud's psychodynamic theories are much more in-depth than this simple analogy.

Greek Mythology

The science of persuasion is not a new concept. Greek mythology provides us with Peitho (*pie tho*), the Goddess of Persuasion. Though in ancient Greece, it was more about the political gains of arranged marriages. Peitho is also seen as the Goddess of Deception and Desire, indicating that trickery marries well with manipulation.

Aristotle's Three Modes of Persuasion

The Greek philosopher, Aristotle, understood the art of manipulation or persuasion very well. He introduced the concept of three modes of persuasion: Ethos, Pathos, and Logos. Don't be put off by the theme of Greek philosophy, because Aristotle had a good insight into how persuasion works. His ideas are still relevant today. To make it relevant to modern society, we will use modern terminology to better explain Aristotle's three modes of persuasion

1 Ethos

Refers to the "character" build of the *influencer*.

The *influencer* feels a need to build up trust in the beginning, to enhance their own credibility. They must appear to be credible so that their intentions are perceived as good. They may even display empathy to falsify that they care for their victim. We can all be persuaded to like someone if they appear to understand us. Once familiarity is in place, we will be more inclined to trust them.

Ethos is all about our own self-portrayal. How we perceive a person looks and speaks will often determine if we feel we can trust them. Once that is in place, it leaves us open to manipulation.

2 Pathos

Refers to the "emotional" exploitation of the influencer, towards their audience.

To elicit the correct emotions from their victim, the persuader needs to fully understand them. By tapping into the victim's emotions, the *influencer* can identify and exploit their target's weaknesses. This vital information will be used by the *influencer*, to manipulate their target. In the early days, the *influencer* will appear understanding so they appeal to the better nature of their victim. The *influencer* is playing and relying on the emotions of their audience, to make them comply.

An example of this can be seen in advertising. An image may be show happy people with a certain type of product. By linking a positive emotion with that product, it will help to sell it. We all want happiness; therefore, we might wish to buy that product.

3 Logos

Refers to logic and facts.

A manipulator is good at providing a cleverness of knowledge, to support an argument. They may reel off lots of statistics and apparent factual detail to impress upon their argument. The likelihood is that the victim will believe them because how can statistics lie? Aren't they proven as a scientific process? The *influencer* may indeed lie about their so-called proof. They are playing with the victim's logic. If they can appear knowledgeable, it makes them convincing. That makes their victim now more open to their manipulation.

A manipulative person will go to great lengths to initially win someone over. By appearing trustworthy and reliable, we are more likely to accept them. For this, they think nothing of substantiating their argument with untruthful facts. Deception and underhand methods are their way of gaining power. The victim has become open to abuse, making it is easy to exploit them.

Now that you are aware of the tactics of a manipulative character, let's have a look at some scientific evidence. This further explains the psychology of manipulative people.

3. Psychology of Manipulation

Who Controls our Lives?

It's interesting to see that manipulation has been around for a long time, and that is not a new or imaginary concept. Understanding what the art of persuasion is really all about is vital, to help you to deal with it.

In this chapter, we will look briefly at the psychology of manipulation. This allows us to see where it might occur in our lives. It will also help you in identifying those who might attempt to manipulate you. It is not only about people who like to dominate. If we don't know it is happening to us, might be encouraged to act in ways that are incongruous to our normal personality and behavior. Learn how commerce can persuade customers into buying their goods and services. Recognizing such methods will help in dealing with the power of persuasion.

We like to believe that we are individuals who make sensible choices. In our personal journey of life, we do not always have full control, and we don't always realize this. As children, we are influenced by our parents and have little control over how we raised. Once in the education system, we are further manipulated. The teachers will tell us all about the social norms and what is expected of us in society. As adults, we are lured in by politicians trying to get their share of votes. Many are persuaded to vote for a party because of what they promise for the future, even if they don't necessarily believe in their policies. This gives such politicians power, and their decisions will affect our lives. Are we really in control of our lives, or are we merely influenced by those who know all the tricks of persuasion?

Later in this book, we will look at how to deal with various manipulative methods, even sometimes covert. First, you need to learn to recognize when you are being manipulated so you can counteract it. For this purpose, we will now look at what the experts say on how this sort of behavior can exist among us.

Recognizing the Art of Manipulation

What then, in our everyday lives, do we need to be wary of?

Persuasive Language

The idiom that every picture tells a story, is very true. Words can be so much more powerful as they inspire and encourage us, even to the point of manipulation. How many times have you been inspired by a good orator, whose daring speech motives you into action? Words even influence when we are lost completely in a great book. The art of words can be so influential in coercing us to believe something, even when our eyes tell us differently. Communication is a powerful tool, especially when it comes to making people do things.

- Advertisers and salespeople use language to convince their goods are just what we are looking for. Using words, such as:

Affordable; Easy to use; Safe; Enjoyable; Time Saving; Guaranteed to last.

Note how all these words make us believe they are confident in their own products.

- Politicians will use language, such as:

"We" - to encompass you in their world.
"Us" to make you feel a part of a team.

These are all communication tactics to make us feel included, so therefore important.

- Bullies use language along with aggressive behavior, to achieve their own selfish goals.

- Criminal predators, such as psychopaths, sociopaths and narcissists, are all people who learn the use of persuasive language. This is a means to get their own way and gain control over another person.

Six Theories on Psychological Manipulation

1 Cognitive

There are many well recognized psychological processes in theories regarding the art of persuasion. One of those is the Cognitive Response model, developed by Anthony Greenwald in 1968. It is still relevant today for determining some factors in persuasion. It is also a model used extensively in the world of advertising.

Greenwald suggested that:

It is not the words of the message that determines the success of persuasion, but more the emotions of the *receiver*. The internal monologue of the one receiving the message will be deciding factor on how easy they are influenced. (2a)

Such internal thoughts will include positive and negative aspects, according to the individual's own personality. This not a learning process, but more based on whether the person already views the message with favorable or unfavorable thought processes (cognitions).

Overcoming any counter-arguments will rely on the expertise of the *persuader*. They should stop their target from having sufficient time to construct any counter-arguments. The *persuader* must encourage positive arguments to come to the forefront. This gives the "persuasion effect" a better chance of success.

Persuasion can be more difficult if the intended target has been forewarned. It allows the target time to build their own counter-arguments, if the "message" is counter-intuitive to their present cognitions. The importance in pre-warning can be seen in research conducted by Richard E. Petty, in 1977. The study showed that students given notice about a certain event were less likely to be persuaded that those who had no pre-warning. (2b)

2 Reciprocity

Another well-studied explanation for how we might be open to the power of persuasion is the Rule of Reciprocity. This is based on a principle related to social conventions. If someone does you a favor, or does something good for you, then you are more likely to feel obliged to return the favor.

The Rule of Reciprocity can also happen subconsciously. Without even realizing it, you may agree to an action or favor asked of you by the requester. All because at some point they had done something for you, and you feel in their debt. You may feel obliged even if the request is something you would normally decline.

It is an effect widely used by companies who are looking to make sales. Often companies give out free samples, or time-limited trials. This is not without a motive. It is in the hope that the customer feels obliged to return the favor, and buy the product or continue with the agreement.

Reciprocity is a recognized psychological process. It is an adaptive behavior which would have increased our chances of survival in the past. By helping others, it is likely that at some later point they will help you. Though, it can also have negative effects. If someone does something bad to you, then you may be driven by the rules of reciprocity to exact your revenge.

The Rule of Reciprocity is well supported by academic research. Burger et al (2009), suggested that a group of participants were more likely to agree to a request if the requester had previously done them a favor. (2c)

3 Information Manipulation

A powerful tool in the manipulator's armory. This is a method of being outright deceitful. It is a means of providing limited and confusing information to the victim. The effect of this will unbalance their way of thinking, making them vulnerable. It can also incorporate the use of intentional body language, to persuade and manipulate someone.

A study by McCornack et al. (1992) (2d) showed the different ways a message can be falsified to assist in the manipulation process. McCornack's theory has a premise of four maxims, in a truthful statement. A breach of any of these will render the message as intentionally deceitful. The four maxims are:

Quantity

This is the "amount" of information provided. Most of us seek to provide the right amount of information so that the receiver understands our message. Not too little, or too much, as that might confuse. A manipulator though would play with that quantity of information. They may omit certain pieces they consider irrelevant. Most especially if it is likely to work against their argument. This is known as "lying by omission."

Quality

Refers to the "accuracy" of the information provided. Truthful communication is one of High Quality. If we were to violate this maxim, then the receiver hears intentional mistruths. This is "outright lying," to gain the manipulator power.

Relation

Here, we talk about the "relevance" of the information to the message. To confuse or sidestep an awkward question, the manipulator may go off topic. This is a way of changing the subject, for the sole purpose of misleading. It could be to hide their own weaknesses. Or even to over-emphasize on something that will give them more power over their listener.

Manner

The "presentation" of the message. An important aspect of this is body language. We read inflections and facial expressions as we listen. A manipulator may exaggerate these to mislead the presentation of the message. This is all in the aim to emphasize their own agenda.

Lying to manipulate or persuade someone is not a new concept. It is though, a method that is becoming particularly potent in the modern world. Online communication and social media do not always involve face-to-face contact. This makes it easier to tell mistruths or exaggerate information. A manipulator may in their elements with such communications.

4 Nudge

Not all manipulation is sinister. Sometimes we may be manipulated to help us make the right decisions for our own good. To do this, the Nudge Theory is particularly useful. The Nudge Theory expands positive reinforcement, by using small nudges.

Skinner's studies or behaviorism, show how useful this theory can be. (2a) With positive reinforcement, such as rewards, it can manipulate people into behaving in the manner that you are hoping to encourage.

One example of "nudging" can be seen in this example. Adding exceptionally high priced items on a menu may seem counterproductive. Yet, the result of this actually increased the sales of the second highest priced item. The customers were given a "nudge" in the right direction, but for the benefit of the restauranteur.

Richard Thaler, considered the father of the Nudge Theory, was awarded the Nobel Memorial Prize in Economic Sciences. (2f) His contribution to behavioral economics was considered quite momentous. Nudge Theory gives positive reinforcement, or as Thaler described it, it gives "nudges."

The Nudge Theory is not only effective in economics. It can be used to encourage behavioral changes and influencing personal choices. Even accepted social norms can be manipulated to changes, in this way.

Nudging is so successful, that in 2010, the British Government set up a Department Behavioral Insights Team. This was to help develop policies. The department was referred to as the Nudge Unit.

There can be obvious benefits of using "nudges" to influence people. It is still a form of psychological manipulation that can infringe on an individual's civil liberties.

5 Social Manipulation

This type of manipulation is also known as psychological manipulation. It is often a tool for politicians, or other groups of powerful people who are used to advancing their own interests. In its worst form, it is a means of social control. By taking away individuality, it coerces the populace into accepting what is given to them. Though it can have a positive side when used to help with personal issues, such as improving health and wellbeing.

Those in power who use social manipulation may use distractive techniques to deflect from important issues. They would argue that their proposals are for the benefit of the populace, and the benefit of your family and its future. Anything you think personally, that might be different, is wrong and selfish. This type of persuasion is very paternalistic, almost treating individuals as if they were all children. This "system" will strive to make the crowds believe the things that have gone wrong are, in fact, their own fault. The only way to resolve the problem is to listen to the guidance of those who know better.

Such a political strategy would bring to forefront one social problem, only to hide another. It is a tactic to cause social unrest and panic among the populace. By creating unease in society, the populace will begin to demand changes. An example could be that the department wishes to hide the problems health care. So, they decrease the budget in crime prevention, causing crime statistics to rocket. The populace will receive information to coerce them into believing the best way forward for the crime problem. The politicians will feed propaganda, by disseminating their own *truths and facts*. It may not always be true, or it may be information that is exaggerated, such as misuse of statistics. This type of social manipulation could take years to get the end result that the manipulator requires.

The use of psychological manipulation is all a part of social influence. Professor Preston Ni, Communication Studies, published an article in Psychology Today. He indicates that *one party recognizes another's weaknesses. They deliberately set out to cause an imbalance of power. This enables them to exploit their victims, for their own agenda.* (2g)

Does this make us all social puppets? To some degree, it does. Most of us comply and conform to what is expected of us to avoid a society of chaos.

Think for a moment, what is the latest gadget or home improvement product that you would like to buy? Is it something a friend told you about, or a neighbor owns? Chances are it is something that someone else has, or you've read that it's popular on the internet, and that makes you desire it. This is another side of social manipulation. We can be so easily swayed if we let our guard down. Whether that is a good or bad thing, depends on how you personally view it.

As mentioned earlier, not all social manipulation is a bad thing. it can have positive aspects. The word "manipulation" might conjure up thoughts of a villainous individual/s bending you to their will. But, used correctly, social manipulation can help the populace, as a whole. Good examples of social manipulation are the "5 a day campaigns." Health specialists attempt to convince us to eat more fruit and vegetables. Or even the "stop smoking campaigns," which have resulted in reduced numbers of smokers. The result of which is a reduction in smoking-related diseases. This is coercion at its best.

6 Gaslighting

This is perhaps the cruelest form of manipulation. It

is a means of casting into doubt on the sanity and self-esteem of a person. You could say it is *sowing the seeds of doubt* into the victim of manipulation. Working on a similar principle such as "knowing you are being told repeated lies." Until eventually you begin to believe the lies as the truth.

It is an unkind form of manipulation. The *gas-lighter* will cause their victim to lose all confidence in their own credibility. This leads to completely destroying their own self-worth. All because they begin to doubt themselves. That is the intention of *gaslighting*, to reduce the victim to a psychological mess. The manipulator will constantly put their target down by contradicting them. Also by convincing them that they are always wrong. Sometimes to the point that the victim will be accused of telling lies. This is why the victim loses all self-esteem. When that happens, they become ruled by the domineering influencer. It is a form of mental abuse, often seen in abusive personal relationships. The influencer will use constant techniques to make their victim doubt themselves. Even to the point of doubting their own memories, by denying things they've said and done.

Gaslighting takes a while before it is fully effective. The manipulator will wear his/her victim down over a long period of time. This type of manipulation is so insidious that it can eventually lead to the victim doubting their own sanity.

Dr. George Simon PhD is a Clinical Psychologist at a Texas university. He has studied people with disturbing personalities. The results of his studies caused him to believe that certain types of personalities, particularly psychopaths, are very adept at manipulation. They will distort the truth and use aggressive language, to set the wheels of doubt in motion in their victim's thoughts. Eventually, the target will lose confidence in their own judgment. They may feel shame and they will come to believe that the manipulator is right. This puts the target under the manipulator's control. (2h)

Gaslighting is not only restricted to individuals acting on one other. It can be argued that it also has political uses. Columnist and author Maureen Dowd is one to follow this belief. She argued that Clinton's administration used gas lighting techniques against a political opponent. Newt Gingrich, a member of the opposing political party, was often goaded into appearing hysterical. Some journalists and psychologists argue that Donald Trump also used gas-lighting techniques. Not only during his presidential campaign but also whilst in office. They argue he frequently says one thing, then denies he ever said it, which is classic gas-lighting. (2i)

4. Language

The Communication Tool

Words are a powerful tool. They can inspire, motivate, and cause us to conjure up images in our imagination. This, in turn, affects our emotions. Imagine then, how powerful that tool is when used by a ruthless manipulator. Those with the skill can build people up to be strong, or knock them down like a set of skittles.

It should be up to us as individuals. Do we allow the words of encouragement or of discouragement, to influence us the most? But, a manipulator will use both methods to gain the end result they are seeking. Initially, they will make their target feel good about themselves. The manipulator now believes the target to be under their persuasion because it is they that have allowed the target to feel that emotion. The target has become a puppet. Once within their grasp, they will seek to break the target's self-esteem. By the sheer power of words, they will break down any self-confidence that they find. All using words. They may even lie to them. Putting them down with sarcasm. Accusing them of being wrong all the time. Both tactics were for the same result. To coerce their target into behaving in a manner that will benefit the manipulator. This is how powerful the art of words can be, and this is in their simplest form.

This maneuver may not appear tangible to the victim. It could be for financial gain, or simply a means to gain control over another person. However, control is achieved, the process will have been devious. Add to that the art of body language, it renders even more power over the use of words. All for the art of persuasion.

Language, as a tool, is one of the fundamental human characteristics that separate us from other living creatures. Even the great apes, our nearest relatives, do not have a grasp of language to the extent that we have. Uniquely, we can use language in an abstract manner. Our minds can create things that do not exist. We can take that a step further and communicate our imaginary thoughts to others. What do you conjure up at the word "alien?" None of us have ever seen one, or at least they are not proven, yet we instantly create an image in our minds.

Different cultures may use different forms of languages to communicate. but language is still used for the same reason, no matter where you are born. It is a way for humans to advance and survive. With language, we can learn much quicker because words give meaning to everything. Words are very influential in conveying how our emotions and our needs.

A manipulator, especially one with no moral boundaries, can use language in a hypnotic way. One such powerful persuasion technique is known as Conversational Hypnosis. A competent proponent of this technique is the ability to manipulate another's thoughts without them even realizing.

For example, someone may be able to convince you to change your mind over a decision. Further, they will make sure that you believe it was your decision to change your mind. You will not even realize that it was they who persuaded you to change your mind.

A study conducted in 2015, looked at relieving anxiety before a medical procedure. The results indicated that Conversational Hypnosis was successful in doing this. (3a)

A similar technique to Conversational Hypnosis is used in a personal development technique. This is known as Neuro-linguistic programming (NLP). (3b). NLP is considered a positive use of the technique. Yet, there are still unscrupulous manipulators who use it to coerce individuals to their own will. This method is subtler, using word deceptions to hide the true intentions. They will attempt to build up a personal trust with their target, albeit on falsities. This bond maneuvers the target into a position to be more agreeable and open to suggestions.

Listening

Language is used for a great many purposes:

- Stories to entertain and educate.
- Lyrics to compliment musical notes.
- Conversations for humans to communicate their emotions to each other.

These are but a few examples but it is the last one that is of interest when we discuss the art of manipulation. Words are a tool, a way of expressing our inner thoughts to others and ourselves. Humans might communicate with language, but words alone are not enough. Words have the power to bring us to our knees and weaken us. They have the power to teach us topics we do not know about or understand, so we can learn and develop. Yet, to know if you can trust what someone is saying is true, there are other factors to consider; body language being one of them. This indicates that language, as powerful as it is, does not work alone in a human relationship. Language can be a potent contrivance, but more information is needed before we can build up our bonds with one another. That is because what a person says with words, may not necessarily reflect the truth of who they are. The ability to perceive fact from opinion is also a useful skill in understanding the communicator's true aims.

What can make words even more powerful is the tone of the user, the inflections in the words they speak. If someone were to ask you to be quiet, in a soft tone, you may or may not take any notice. If there is a menace to the tone of their soft words, then you are more likely to pay attention. If they shouted the words at you, then you might take more note of the request. If the tone is one of uncertainty in their authority, then maybe not. Whether others take note of the spoken request or instructions, could be dependent on how influential that person is. If it is a person perceived as authoritative, such as a teacher to a student, then words will have meaning. If the words are spoken from someone unknown, then the words are less likely to have any influence. This means that the same words can be used by different people, and result in different effects. It is not only the power of the word, but the power of the user to that transfers the message across.

Inner Voice

We can also use words to communicate with ourselves. We may write a journal, or have a discussion with ourselves in our own mind. For some, this is a great form of therapy. It can even help us to problem solve, by visually mind mapping a solution to some difficulty we are experiencing. Or, it can help us to maintain a good balance of mental health, by writing down our emotions. We are still using words, and playing the role of our own counselor to comfort ourselves in times of stress.

Social Interactions

But, humans are social creatures and prefer to share words. Using language as a means of understanding our environment. There are few humans who prefer the solitary life of their own company to that of others. Most of us like to be with other people. The use of language will help build up friendships and share common interests. None of us need to be experts in linguistics to achieve this goal. Body language also comes into play. Observation compliments language. Combined it gives us efficient feedback on whether we will feel safe of who we are with.

We are at ease if we are in a group of like-minded people. Why then would anyone connect themselves with people who make them feel uncomfortable? Yet, we do. It could be that we have been fooled into believing a false impression. It is easy to use the combination of words and body language to mislead someone. Most of us would not wish to use such tactics, but there are many that would have no scruples about doing so.

5. Character Traits of a Manipulator

Is language the primary tool of deviously manipulative people? How can words have such a powerful effect on us?

How a manipulative person mind works, is most likely only something a manipulative person could comprehend. The rest of us look on in confusion, wondering why or how someone could behave this way. Though, in some small way, we can all be a little manipulative at times. For example, most people will be willing to bend the truth, or omit information, on the odd occasion. For much the same reasons, such as trying to get others to do something for them or even to get permission for something. Trying to convince someone of your argument or to get them to come around to your way of thinking, is a natural and evolutionary process. Pinker and Bloom (1990) argued that we evolved to use language because it helped us to adapt to our environments (4a). Surviving hostile elements is easier if we can persuade others to help us persevere.

The use of language to manipulate others to help us is the evolutionary adaptation, appears to be a natural process. Why then, do some individuals manipulate others for more perversive means? Not for survival or evolutionary means, but purely for their own selfish needs. If they cannot achieve this control, they feel helpless and lack any agency in their lives. Why? Are they evil, are they unkind, are they born that way? Some might say it is a personality disorder that is bordering on a narcissistic level.

We will all try to persuade someone at some point in our lives, but we are not all narcissists. Whatever the reason for our attempts at persuasion, we usually want to remain on good terms with the person we are trying to manipulate. Not so for those who manipulate to control.

Kier Harding, a lead Mental Health practitioner, wrote a relevant article in The Diagnosis of Exclusion. He argued that those diagnosed with a personality disorder are actually people who are not very good at manipulating. (4b) Their attempts tend to be forceful and over exaggerated. Whereas a skillful manipulator will aim to persuade someone less overtly. It is because they are not very good at it, that makes them unlikable characters with poor interpersonal skills. Usually also with a low self-esteem because of their background in life. This could be an argument indicating that controlling manipulators are from dysfunctional backgrounds.

How then can we recognize such a deviant person?

Common Traits

Use of Language

We have shown how powerful language can be, as a prime tool of persuasion. There is more to the manipulative controller though than mere words. They will use tactics that mislead and unbalance their target's inner thoughts. We now understand that through language, they will:

- Use mistruths to mislead and confuse their target's normal thinking pattern.
- Force their target to make a decision at speed, so they don't have time to analyze and think.
- Talk to their target in an overwhelming manner, making them feel small.
- Criticize their target's judgment so they begin to lose their own self-esteem.
- Raise the tone of their voice and not be afraid to use aggressive body language.
- Ignore their target's needs, they are only interested in getting what they want and at

any cost.

Invasion of Personal Space

Most of us set boundaries around ourselves without realizing we are doing so. It is a kind of unspoken rule to protect our own private space, such as not sitting so close that you are touching another person, especially a stranger. A manipulative character cares nothing about overstepping such boundaries. Whether this is because they do not understand, or they do not care is unclear. Initially, they are unlikely to invade their target's personal space. They will seek to build up a good rapport first. This shows that they do understand boundaries because once they gain the confidence of their target, they will then ignore them.

Fodder for Thought

Manipulators tend to be very ego-centric, with limited social skills. Their only concern is for themselves. Everything they do in life will be in relation to how it affects them, not how their actions affect others. Does this mean that they have a psychopathic disorder?

Take empathy for instance. Controlling manipulators are unlikely to ever show empathy. Empathy is a natural human emotion that aids in our survival techniques. A study by Meffert et al. indicates that those with a psychopathic disorder are able to control empathetic emotions (4c). They lack sympathy of any kind because another weakness is simply another tool for them. When they detect any weakness in their target's resolve or personality, they will exploit it. The consequences to their victim are of little importance. The targets weakness's feed the manipulator's strength, making them bolder and often crueler in their actions.

Creating Rivalry

Another tactic of the controlling manipulator is backstabbing. They may tell you how great a person you are to your face, making themselves look good. Behind your back, they are busy spreading malicious gossip and untruths about you. This is a classic trait of a controlling manipulator as it creates a rivalry between people. Then, they can pick sides that will make them look favorable, particularly to their target. It can act as the first stage to getting close to their target. Once bonded, they can start to build up trust, making it easier to manipulate the target in the future. If you recognize a backstabber, keep them at a distance. Their agenda is selfish so it is better not let them into your personal life. There is no point treating them as they treat you, in revenge. It will turn out to be exhausting playing them at their own game. If they know that you are on to them, they may attempt to lure you back with praise, remember that it is false.

Domineering Personality

It is unlikely that a manipulative person will outwardly show any form of weakness. An important part of their facade is to show conviction about their views. They seek to impress, believing they are right about everything. Almost to the point that if they realize they are wrong, they will still argue that they are right. On a one-to-one level, that invariably means that your position is always wrong. As they will chip away at your beliefs, they seek to undermine your sense of self-esteem. Once they have achieved this, then there is no holding them back. They seek to domineer others, often speaking with a condescending tone to belittle their victims. Using ridicule is yet another tool against their target, merely because it will make themselves look better. If you ridicule them back, they will seek to turn the tables, accusing you of being oversensitive to their "joke." The kind of joke that only the teller sees the funny side.

Passive Aggressive Behavior

A common trait of many hard-core manipulators is passive aggressive behavior. Because they prefer to be popular, they do not wish to be seen as doing anything wrong. Not that a manipulator would ever admit to doing anything wrong. They are experts with facial expressions that are meant to dominate and intimidate. This may include; knitting eyebrows, grinding teeth and rolling eyes. It may also include noises such as tutting and grunting sounds. It is a very common behavior for such a character, as there is little anyone else has to say that they will agree upon. For most manipulators, it is their life's ambition to show people up by proving them wrong.

This can range from the confrontational look, where they seek to stare their target down. Or, It could be in response to their disagreement on something their target said. They may smirk and shake their head, turn their back, anything to show their strong disapproval. It is all a ploy to make themselves look superior and put others down.

Moody Blues

What of emotional stability of the manipulator? Is it that which makes them behave the way they do? Do they even know what happiness is? The answer to that is a most definite yes, at least to the latter.

Happiness is a tool used initially to help them manipulate, a happy target is more likely to comply. This, in itself, makes the manipulator happy, or at least in a sense of what they consider happiness. But their joyfulness is a perverted model of what most others consider happiness to be. Their happiness is often built on the foundations of another's misery. A misery that they have caused with their cruel manipulations. Equally though, a manipulator is prone to mood swings. Most likely to happen when things are not going to plan. One minute they are euphoric at their latest conquest. Then next they could be completely deflated at their failure to succeed. One thing is certain for those who live with or become a target of this type of domineering character, they will be unhappy all the time.

Intimidation

One aspect of manipulation, often used as a last resort, is intimidation and bullying. When everything else has failed, they begin to use threats to get their own way. Some though may use intimidation from the onset. It may in a source of authority. For example, let's take the role of a manipulative boss. You have requested a day off. They don't want to allow you your request but have no choice, it is your right. This type of person would want their pound of flesh first. They will set goals for you to reach so it will delay or cancel your request, such as moving project deadlines forward. This way they have their little victory over you.

Alternatively, such a manipulator may use the tactic of the silent treatment. Ignoring someone to the point that it becomes obvious you have displeased them. They seek to make you feel the guilty party.

Other more direct intimidating actions may include stance. Using their height or build to tower over you, or standing uncomfortably close.

Be careful as they will seek revenge for wrongdoings they perceive done to them. Nothing will go unnoticed under their watchful eye. Everyone is a potential target. But, the weak are more likely to walk into their traps, because they are the ones who are easier to dominate. The vulnerable will have little resistance and are easier to bully and coerce. Many of these traits seem more fitting to men, but women can be cruelly manipulative too.

This is a person who will never back down in an argument. Never admit they are wrong. Never apologize for anything. A manipulator will never show respect but will expect everyone else to show them respect.

They love nothing more than to embarrass others. Playing the dumb one is common practice, just to force another person to explain themselves further. At every opportunity, the manipulator will jump in with some sarcastic remark, "hurry up, we're all waiting for your intellectual explanation," or "why has no one else ever heard of this?" Their sole aim is to make the other person look a fool, but without seeming to be the one who made it happen. *Oh no, the victim did that to themselves because they are stupid.*

So, what of the victims of such a manipulator? Let's now move on to the other side of this role.

6. Victims of Manipulation

Three ways of becoming the victim of a controlling manipulator

We have looked at the character of the controlling manipulator, but what of their victims, how do they become ensnared? It might surprise you how much we are all manipulated in our daily lives.

There are the situations where any one of us could find ourselves being easily persuaded. Every day we are bombarded with advertisements, all urging us to buy their wares. Extolling the virtues of one product over another. Building a discourse where not buying certain goods is almost seen as unthinkable, out of sync with the zeitgeist.

1. Sales Tactics

This is the obvious example of such a situation. It seems to be the acceptable face of social manipulation. Commercial products always seem to carry some type of manipulative tactic. All in aid of getting the public to buy the goods. The worse of it is that we are aware of the scheming maneuvers, and yet we still fall prey to them.

When marketing is done well, it works. That's why advertising is a multi-million dollar enterprise. Companies do not have huge advertising budgets for no reason. For example, how often do we succumb to their, "Buy One Get One Free" offers or half price sales? (5a). They seem like a real bargain, saving our hard-earned bucks. Often, we are coerced into buying products we might not even need or ever wanted in the first place. The offer tempts us with generous words, such as "Free" or "Reduced." Yet, it is a marketing ploy to manipulate customers to empty out their purses and wallets. It even has its own acronym, known as BOGOF. Customers are seduced by attractive false pretenses. Are the stores or companies really being kind in giving us free products? How can they afford to that? The truth of it is that they are not giving anything away for free.

Economist, Alex Tabbarok,* informs us that there are many ways that these offers can seduce us. The cost of a product is seemingly reduced, giving the customer an offer that's too good to refuse. Most likely the price of the product is increased prior to the offer, so the customer pays more in the first place. (5a) Most larger shops buy their goods in bulk. This means that the price they pay for an individual product is far less than the price they charge their customers. That is acceptable because they are a business after all, and must make profits to keep going.

You may also note that the BOGOF temptation is used on a lot of perishable items. If the stores have a surplus and the sell-by date is fast approaching, it makes commercial sense to reduce the price, or use BOGOF. If you are coerced into buying this type of bargain, make sure you can eat it all before it expires. Some have argued that this practice of promotion has led to an increase in food waste. The stores and shops refute this theory completely.

Such commercial practices are seen as choices that adults can assess intelligently. No one is forcing us to participate in the offers. We all have individual agency and should take responsibility for our actions. Yet, somehow, we are blinded to the persuasiveness of such marketing methods.

We live in a consumerist society. The need to own the latest gadget or have the latest model can become crucial to the buyer. Not only for their standing in society but also their sense of self. Advertisers take advantage of our weak areas and offer us unmissable deals at supposedly low rates. If customers cannot afford it, no problem, they will be offered credit for their purchase.

It should come as no surprise that advertising has such a powerful impact on our lives. Linked to the massive increase in consumerism over the last few decades, is a similar increase in marketing efforts. In the 1970's, it was believed that the average person viewed around 500 adverts, that has now increased to 5000 ads, in a single day. Whilst that might seem excessive and may not apply to everyone, it does show the pervasive nature of advertising in everyday life (5b). Advertising is proven to work, overtly manipulating the shopper and often tagging into their emotions to coercing them to purchase the product in question. Though it may not work every time and on every person, it is successful often enough to make it a profitable venture.

Of course, no one is physically or mentally abusing customers, or attempting to ruin their lives. It is a business tactic, not a personal ploy. Even though it is done subtly, it can have a powerful effect on the lives and wellbeing of individuals.

Some people are far more vulnerable to manipulation than others. Some are very impressionable, and sometimes vulnerable too. A classic target for scammers and strong-armed sales personnel, are the elderly. They are easy to confuse when a strong character is knocking on their door. This part of the population is perfect for the controlling manipulator. Their weaknesses can be taken advantage of. Such people will not fully comprehend what is being put to them. Even if they do understand, they may fear to say "no." That makes them the perfect target for unscrupulous manipulators.

2. Working Environment

Anyone who is vulnerable is a potential target of a manipulator. It is not always the obvious people that can get ensnared. Already we have learned that such a character will initially behave with impeccable manners. This false front is performed to impress and gain trust. If you do not know this person already, it may be hard to recognize that you have become their target. That is until it is too late. On a personal front, this type of relationship can occur at work, or even in intimate relationships.

Consider your place of work. Do you have a boss that makes your life a misery by demanding work at higher and quicker levels constantly? Browbeating you to meet impossible targets. Warning you of a reduction in your salary or canceling any bonuses. Could even threaten to sack you. At that point, you become trapped. This person knows we all have responsibilities, such as mortgages or rents and families to support. We cannot walk away. In such a situation, any of us could become this vulnerable person. This is the victim of a controlling manipulator.

Here are some typical manipulative tactics of this character. See if any of the sound familiar in your current work situation. "Carreerizma" is a career website that provides useful guidance and resources. In a relevant blog article, they cover this exact topic (5c).

• Fake Praise

The boss said they liked your idea and think you're a great person, but then they go with someone else's idea instead. What was the point of the pretense in the first place? Like many manipulators, they like the feeling of control. By leading you astray, it gives them a sense of power over you. This is about building a person's confidence up with false praise, and then crushing them. At this point, they may belittle you or devalue your work. Diving in with the kill to make you feel worthless. Now they have you like a puppet under their control.

• Stealing the credit of your talents

Using you to write up their own reports, then taking all the credit for it. This is a classic manipulative strategy. They tell you that you're perfect for the job. Show you how they trust in you as the best person to get the job done. All that encouragement was a complete front for their real plans. Once the job is completed, they claim any praise for themselves. Now you are left on the sideline, feeling well and truly exasperated. Should you question them about it, they'll claim your report was a total mess. It's better now because they spent all morning putting it right.

• Embarrassing you

Putting people down, in front of others, makes these characters feel powerful. Say that you put forward an idea, they may laugh and ridicule the very thought of it. After a while, you no longer believe in it yourself. Were you to confront them about their behavior, they' would come back at you with sarcasm, "Hell, man, can't you take a joke?" Cruel jokes and sarcasm, all will be done at your expense.

• Blame shifting

Whatever has gone wrong is everyone else's fault, but theirs. Never would they admit up to their own shortcomings and mistakes. Not only that, they'll often deny any negative things they might have done. Should you attempt to explain the wrong they did, they would only claim that your version of events is wrong. Typically, they will say, '*I don't normally behave like that, only when I'm around you.*" This is what Freud called projection. They are projecting their own misdemeanors onto someone else.

• Belittling
Making others feel irrelevant. Such as, if you walk into their office they don't stop whatever they're doing to greet you. Instead, you get a wave of the hand to come in. They know you are there, but take an age to get to you. It leaves you sitting there feeling insignificant, which is exactly how they want you to feel.

Quite often they will bring irrelevant information into an argument, especially if they are losing. Moving goalposts whilst in a discussion is a classical way to make themselves look good. These people must have the last word, always.

Unappreciative of anything you do and pushing you to your limits are all signs to watch out for. If you hear these bells, you are working for a manipulative controller.

Working with such people can be a game of survival and not everyone has the strength of character to win. Some, once they've identified them, will stay clear of such people. Their tactic is to keep them out of their lives by avoiding them. That can be difficult if the person doing the manipulation is your employer or your partner. Others may stand up to them and confront them. This is risky but done in the right way could result in the manipulator moving on to another target. Most of the time we have no choice other than to put up with them. We all have our own strategies on how to deal with people we don't like, but the handling of a narcissistic manipulator takes courage. You are not alone and our last chapter will guide you in taking the necessary steps.

Working with a controlling figure can make your life unhappy, living with one can make your life hell. Have a look at some of the signs to look out for, to know if you are in such a relationship.

3. Personal Relationships

This is a terrible situation to find yourself in. Being in a relationship whereby your supposedly loving partner keeps you on a leash. When someone wants to control everything that you do, it can become a dangerous situation to find yourself in. This type of partner might tell you it's for your own good. They are keeping you safe, under their protective wing. Yet, being on the other end of such treatment does not feel safe. It is a suffocating experience that comes with other serious problems, such as sexual, physical and mental abuse.

Signs of a Manipulative Partner

Let's look at some examples of how manipulation manifests itself in personal relationships (5d).

Perhaps you can see some of these traits in yours?

- Manipulators are always control-freaks. The more control they have, the more they sink their teeth into the victim.

- They will violate other people's personal boundaries. It could come in the form of snooping and spying, or even more bold open actions. To enable them to do this, you will be allowed nothing personal, such as your phone or computer. They will pry your passwords from you, in some sly way. At the same time, they jealously guard their own boundaries, being the first to complain if their personal space is breached.

- They may force your hand, such as stopping you from seeing your own friends. They do not want to share what is theirs, and you are their property. To start with they will show you that they don't like your friends. Inside, they see them as a threat. Jealousy is taken to the extreme and may even become aggressive.

- If you make a decision without them, they will not be happy. They don't want you to have free will, otherwise one day that decision may be to leave them!

- Their control may appear in the form of advice, though you have little or no choice but to accept it. They are not advising you, they are instructing you in what to do, and how to behave.

- It is not unusual, in fact, it is usually essential that a manipulative partner will want to know your daily routine. Step out of that routine, and they will interrogate you for it.

- You may notice that they often criticize anything you say, particularly in public. Belittling your opinions and thoughts gives them a sense of, "they know best." Another means of imposing their power over you.

- Not only do they enjoy putting you down, but they may go the extra mile. Accusing you of lying or having a bad memory, or even having the cheek to call you the manipulator.

- You can never please a controlling

manipulator. If you think you have got to that point, they move their own goal posts. This is a relationship whereby you never know exactly where you stand.

If you are in a manipulative and abusive relationship, then no doubt it will be an unhappy one. Manipulators can be very unpredictable. Often, they turn to rage at what they see as a violation of their rules.

It is not easy to break out of such a relationship, but there are some agencies that can help. When you can do this safely, search the web for local organizations that assist victims of abusive partners. Don't forget to delete your browsing history because nothing is private from a manipulator. The stress in on your own safety, but you must seek that help. Our last chapter will give you more guidance on how to build up courage, because the chances are that you are now a quivering wreck.

Know When You Are the Target

Financial Gain

This is one of the major motives for manipulation. That motive is not only limited to the commercial world. Manipulation in a personal relationship may be for financial reasons too. It could come in the form of family trying to force an elderly relative to change their will in their favor. Even an abusive partner who controls everything about your life, including your personal finances.

Sexual Gain

For some, there is a sexual element to their manipulation. They use their overpowering control over their victims to gain sexual favors. Some may even use physical force, in effect rape, to satisfy their sexual urges. Others may be subtler in their approach. This can begin in the form of extreme praise and flattery, lavishing their target with gifts and false promises. They will come across as the perfect attentive partner. Watch out! Once they have you where they want you, they can quickly turn too controlling, and even become violent. It is their goal to keep you trapped in the relationship. Emotional blackmail is their game. The use of fear begins, making you feel obliged and guilty for not complying to their requests.

A person prepared to put another through hell for their own gratification is someone to be reviled. As discussed already, most manipulators suffer severe psychological problems, which make them act as they do.

- The Anti-social personality will display little empathy and have an exaggerated sense of self-worth.

- The narcissistic personality disorder has a great need to control others. This hides their own defects.

- The sadistic personality enjoys inflicting psychological as well as physical pain on others.

One thing they all have in common is to gain absolute power over other people's lives. That, in itself, gives them great pleasure.

Considering that most manipulators have damaged personalities, should we pity them? Should we try to help them?

The best answer to both those questions is a big, "No." Pity only motivates them further. You cannot help them, only they can help themselves by admitting that they have a problem in the first place. They must identify their own weaknesses, which is a highly unlikely action of such a character.

The following chapter is intended to guide you on

how to deal with a manipulative relationship, whether personal or work related.

7. Ten Tips for Dealing with Manipulative People

Here we arrive at the core of the book:

How to stand up against a controlling manipulative person?

1 Ground rules.

- What you have read so far will help you to identify the difference between persuasion and manipulation. Persuasion may be for yours or the teams own benefit, manipulation is always for the controller's benefit. Examples could be: is what you are being asked to do within your normal remit? Are they asking you to rush something through for the team, or for their own personal remit? Will this benefit you, or make you look bad? Do you like and trust this person?

- Manipulative people can seem to be

everywhere. Most manipulation is not necessarily oppressive. Not every stranger asking you to do something is a controlling manipulative person.

- Everyone can be a little manipulative when they need to be, so not every manipulative person is bad.

- Take your time to identify a person whom you suspect to be a control freak. Do they come across as selfish? Are they approachable? Do they seem excessively bossy?

There are ways you can deal with a manipulator, should you have the misfortune to meet one.

2 Observe a manipulator before you label them.

It is not unusual in a workplace to have people

telling you what to do. So long as they ask in the correct manner and they have the authority. Authority comes in many guises. It could be because they are your managers, or they are close work colleagues. If the request is genuine, then it should not be a problem. If someone is constantly demanding you to do things with aggressive coercion, then you are right to be suspicious. Don't jump the gun though, take your time. You don't want to overreact and ruin a workplace relationship unnecessarily.

Observe their behavior whenever you can, without them realizing what you are doing. Keep your distance because you don't want to attract this character's attention. It is important to identify this person for what they are, so you to keep them at a distance in the future.

How then do you handle them when you have to be in their presence?

3 Never let them see your own weaknesses.

If you recognize someone to be a controlling manipulative person, it might be best that you have as little contact with them as possible. This can be difficult in a working environment, but try to restrict personal contact with them. That way, you are not likely to ever divulge your personal life or any problems you may be having. The last thing you want is for them to recognize any of your own weaknesses. They may use that information to gain a hold over you.

Example: You accidentally ate someone else's yogurt in the kitchen area, at work. It was a genuine mistake, you thought it was yours. The owner of the yogurt kicks up a fuss about who has "stolen" their yogurt. You want to admit it, but you keep your head down and stay quiet. Unfortunately for you, the manipulative person saw you eating the yogurt. The likelihood is that they will not give you away, but instead store the information away. At some point in the future, they will tell you that they kept your secret. This is an innocuous example, but it shows how easy it is to become ensnared by a manipulative individual. It is from such humble beginnings that an expert manipulator is able to get under your skin. Once in their clutches, it can be hard to break away.

The best option is to be open and honest. If you can handle your own weaknesses, then how can a control freak find a hold on you?

4 Never allow them to put you down, especially in front of others.

A common psychological phenomenon often exploited by manipulator's is Imposter syndrome. This is a phenomenon that has been well studied. At least 70% of people will suffer from Imposter syndrome at some time in their life (6a). It includes that dreaded feeling of inadequacy at whatever you attempt to do. Even if there is evidence that shows you otherwise, such as your own success at your work. You feel a fraud and you are simply waiting for someone to announce it. That someone may very well be the office manipulator. Except, of course, they are not uncovering you because you are perfectly proficient at your job. What they are actually doing is working on your own feelings of inadequacy. It's how manipulators work, especially the more invasive ones.

When you stand up to a manipulator, they can become abusive. A forceful manipulator will not let people stand in the way of their primary objective. Everyone is fair game in their attempts at power-play. If there is one in your work environment, it will only be a matter of time before they turn their attention to you.

What can you do?

- Show them your confident side, especially if this person is constantly putting people down.

You know them for what they are.

- Convince yourself that anything they say is untrue.

- Do not allow them to break you, and do not bend to their will. Try not to be confrontational with them, that could make matters worse, but stand up for yourself.

- Sometimes, the best strategy is to take it on the chin, and walk away. If their schemes and plans do not affect you, they will soon lose interest.

- Don't bluster in front of them, that is a sign of weakness.

- Show your strengths and the attitude that you

have no care about what they think or say.

- Then pat yourself on the back and walk away.

- It is important that any conversation you have with them is never on a personal level. They may try to make it personal but you must steer them away.

If someone does not treat you with respect, then show your contempt in a respectful way. Then, turn your back on them.

If someone is making unreasonable demands of you, stay clear of them whenever you can. If you can't meet their needs and they complain, be brave. Explain the truth of the situation but not in a defensive manner. Try not to be hostile or confrontational in any way, but don't allow them to walk all over you.

If you are successful at rebutting their attempts to manipulate you, they may become aggressive and personal. Now they may attempt the Imposter syndrome. This is where the insults of incompetent, inadequate and useless may come at you. Keep your calm and keep a distance of space between you. Don't apologize, that's what they want you to do. Trust in your own instincts and advise them to go to your supervisor with their complaints. If they are your supervisor, then let them know that you may need to take this further up the ladder of management. If you say this with commitment, they may falter. If you say it with fear, it may be time to walk away and indicate that you will speak with them once they calm down.

If the situation gets to this point, you may want to find someone you can trust to help you calm down. Tell them what happened so you can get it off your own chest. It was a disturbing situation, but you must be able to move on from it. Don't brood and don't be fearful of them.

They may not calm down and start making you a target of their abuse. Now is the time to be looking at making that complaint to those in a higher authority. Before you do that, begin to document your evidence of any future events involving you both. This will provide you with evidence for the day you decide to go ahead and report them. Whether your boss will accept your complaint is irrelevant. You have evidence to back up your argument and it could be enough for the manipulator to back off. Sadly, they will only find someone else to pick on unless the senior management accepts that there is a problem.

If you are regularly under the spell of a narcissistic manipulator, then will have low self-esteem. You MUST build up your self-confidence and become more powerful within yourself. Only then will you be able to break the chains they have wrapped around you.

5 How to leave a control freak

For many people, especially women, this can happen in the family home. For such victims, trying to break free is the most difficult. Not the least because the victim may, in fact, love their toxic partner or parent. If you are in such an unhappy situation then you must consider your own wellbeing and safety. Only if the perpetrator can admit that they have a problem and seek help, can they begin to mend. If they learn to compromise and accept your input, then it will be a great step forward. Such an openness may save a two-way partnership. The problem is though, such a manipulator cannot see that they are making your life a misery. If they are so blind, how can they ever accept that something is wrong? Indeed, if you approach them they may become defensive and aggressive. This is because they perceive you as having insulted their integrity and pride. How dare you accuse them of anything!

Unfortunately, if you are in such a relationship then

the only way you will be free is to make the break yourself. The adage, *"You only have this one life, live it to the fullest,"* is never apter than in this situation.

How though, do you find the courage to leave? That is exactly what it will take to be rid of such an overpowering partner. They may even continue to threaten you after you have dared to leave. That is one of the reasons why you dare not make that move.

How then do you build up your confidence to finally leave the relationship?

6 Begin with building up a support network.
It is vital that you have support from friends and family. This can be a difficult one though. It could be that the very partner you have just left, browbeat you to severing all personal ties. If this is your

situation and you are unable to pick up those ties, then there are organizations that you can turn to. These agencies can guide you on dealing with your situation.

It is going to be a rough ride and you may even need a safe house where your partner does not know where to find you. Don't feel ashamed. If you have children it will be even harder, but for their sakes, get them away. They can make contact again in later years if they so wish. Then they may better understand what happened. Bear this in mind that if you feel stifled, then almost certainly they do too.

That is, of course, the worst scenario. No matter how hard it is for you to leave, you must take the time for yourself, and recoup.

7 Don't forget your own health needs.

Do things that help you relax, if possible. Get outside and take short walks. You need personal space so you can consider your situation. Listening to music you like or immersing yourself in a book or a TV program, is good if it helps you to switch off. Avoid overeating or drinking too much alcohol. Your problem will become tenfold if you take that route. All these points are double stressed if you have children. You need to stay strong for them, and for yourself.

8 Accept that you will feel scared.

If your partner has sensed anything, they could revert to being overly nice to you. Don't be fooled, you know without anyone having to tell you that it will not last. It will only be natural to hesitate in your actions, whether it is out of fondness, pity, or fear. Fear of being on your own is natural. Fear of your partner's violence is not. If that's something you feel, then you are most certainly making the right choice. If you do leave, then you must make it quick and clean, leaving no trace of where you are going. Manipulative, obsessive partners will attempt to track down fleeing partners, even if only to punish them. You have broken their self-ego and now they have no one left to control. If they do find you, they may try the extra-nice approach and beg you to return, or they may be violent and angry. You don't want to be there for any confrontations whatsoever.

If possible, then make a complete break and move to a new city. I know this might not seem practical and a little extreme, but you do want to bump into such an ex-partner. Most cities and large communities have agencies to help victims of domestic violence, to start afresh. It won't be easy but it will be worth it. Consider all your options before you put your plan in motion, because you may need to be tucked away for a while.

9 What are the after stages?

Once you make the break, accept that it is

permanent. This one chance may be the only opportunity you get. Everyone's motives and decisions for making such a daring move are individual choices. It can be especially difficult if children are involved. Often, those who have managed to make the break can eventually give in. It could be out of a sense of pity, or a false sense of being beholden. The controlling partner will offer to change their ways, and could even manage to do it, but most do not. You may give in thinking they cannot live without you around to help them. This is a form of pity and you should fight it off. If you give in, you will go right back to square one. Be selfish and think about yourself for a change. Perhaps you might feel lonely and that in retrospect life together wasn't that bad. This is a natural reaction at first, but tell yourself, if it had not been that bad, why did you leave?

Remember that your own confidence will still be at a low level, even if you managed to leave the abusive relationship. It is going to take time to heal, as any injury does. Get to know your own self once again. You have lost touch with your own needs and what you desired out of life before your relationship. You need time so you can build up your own self-esteem and find out what you want out of your new life. It may take years before you recover, so be patient with yourself.

You may lack the courage to face a world that suddenly seems huge and overwhelming. Compounding that is the fact that you might not even have yourself a home, once you leave. That should be your priority, searching for a place you can call home, somewhere you will feel safe. Finding employment, or schools for the children can follow. These can all be remedied in time, so don't expect all the answers immediately.

Eventually, you will begin to trust yourself and believe in your own decisions. Make sure you do things that you enjoy, even if it is only reading a book. Your mind needs to adjust to this strange independence you have gained. You may even feel lost without having someone to make all the decisions for you. Allow yourself time, that is all it takes.

Don't worry if you don't make friends very easy; you have been out of the loop for a long time. Anyway, you need to pick and choose your new friendships carefully. The last thing you want is to meet another domineering personality. It may result in a few trust issues on your part, but that is not important. You have every right to be cautious.

10 Build up your courage.

Once you have built up your courage and self-esteem, you can then face the world head-on. We all approach this one in a different way. The first rule must be, not to compare yourself to others. It is not an easy rule to follow, but nonetheless, you are new to freedom. That is exactly what you are, free.

Forget other people. Of course, be polite, but concentrate on your needs and not anyone else's, unless you have children.

There will come a time when you must begin to take risks. That is after the huge risk you have put yourself through by leaving. You have taken a huge leap forward, no need to jump in feet first, give it time to settle.

A great exercise for those who are worriers, is to write down all the worst situations you feel may befall you. Once you have a thorough list, the next stage is to consider how you might deal with each of them. Take notes on your best plan and strategy. This will show you the problem from a detached perspective. It will help you determine which approach is best for each situation. If you feel it is too overwhelming, then break it down into smaller and more manageable steps. As you tackle each micro-step, before you know it, you will have reached the last one. Baby steps do lead to resolving the whole of the problem.

You will make mistakes! the proverb, "to err is human," is true. You need to embrace any mistakes you make and learn by them Learning the right way to do something is so much easier when you have knowledge of the wrong way. You're not perfect, no one is, but you only need to be as perfect as you yourself want to be.

8. Do We All Have a Dark Side?

Throughout this book, we have talked about what a manipulative person is capable of doing. Also mentioned was the fact that we can all be a little manipulative if we need something. Does this mean that we all have a dark side to our character?

Our Own Dark Side

- Why do we enjoy scary or violent movies?
- Why do we gossip, become judgemental, lose our tempers or be downright selfish sometimes?
- Why do we have bad thoughts when we believe we are good deep down?

Case Scenario:

- Let's assume when you were younger, your peer group dared you to steal something from a shop.

- You did not want or even need the item, but you wanted your peer group to like you.
- As an adult, you feel ashamed of that dishonesty, whether you got away with it or not.
- To cover our mistake over, we may begin to tell lies.
- Our minds then go to the extent of attempting to repress the memory, so we don't have to deal with our shame on a daily basis.
- We live with a fear of being exposed, in case we are rejected for our unsavory behavior.

It's doubtful there is anyone who has ever lived that does not have some embarrassing secret they hide from others.

- What then, if there are many shameful experiences in your past that you are unable to suppress?

This can lead to stress and depression, which in turn can lead to medication, alcohol, drugs and even addiction. Not that these are reasons for addiction, but our dark side can be a strain on our lives. It can mold us into characters that are false to our true soul.

Dark Psychology

Dark psychology relates to the unethical ways that people can use to get what we want.

- Have you ever lied or exaggerated on your CV to get a job?

Sounds innocent enough, but it is a means of dark manipulation to get what you desire. It is a dark tactic used purposefully to mislead another person. We learn from a young age how to get our own way by using manipulative tactics. Some children may throw tantrums if they don't get their own way. Is that not a means of attempting to manipulate their parents? If the parent gives in to the tantrum, the child may repeat this in the future. Have they have learned the art of manipulation? It seems uncomfortable to accuse children of dark manipulation, but are we born with such skills, or do we learn them?

A new-born baby cries for the attention of its parent, could we accuse a baby of manipulative behavior? Sounds a little unethical to accuse a baby of using dark psychology, but some would argue that it is true. The baby has to survive, so cries out to get what it needs.

Here we arrive at the Nature v Nurture argument.

Cognitive Skills

This includes our mental ability to think and learn. The part of our brain that gives us this individuality lays in the prefrontal cortex, but it develops as we age. Studies show that it is not fully developed until we reach our twenties (7a).

A child cannot understand they are using manipulation to get what they want. Their brain is not capable of plotting such dark thoughts, because it is not yet developed enough. It is the baby's fear that causes it to cry out, not a profound means of plotting and planning. You could describe it better as a primitive response in a child, to cry out. They do not understand what they want or need. They only know that they need something, and they have learned to trust their parents to soothe them. A child has not learned to understand their emotions. As they enter emotional distress, the brain will trigger chemicals and hormones. Surely then it nature responding. In effect, the child has lost control and does not understand why they feel as they do.

This is not a book about how to deal with unruly

children, but it cannot be denied that their cognitive skills are underdeveloped. Much can be said as to why teenagers act as they do. Often alienating themselves with their unsocial behavior. It is all a learning process. They need good teachers and good role models so they develop into healthy caring adults.

Persuasion v Manipulation

Robin Dreeke, FBI Head of Behavioral Analysis (2013), discussed persuasion v manipulation in an interview with "Psychology Today. In his view, "The difference between persuasion and manipulation is intent." He goes on to suggest that, persuasion is more about empowering the other person with choices. Even in the art of sales persuasion is a better tactic than manipulation. If you give the customer choices, and they chose not to buy your goods, at least they leave you knowing that you gave them control of their decision. The chances are they will remember this kind of respect. They may well return, knowing that you treated them fairly. Had you used manipulative tactics, and they still had not bought your goods, they may leave full of guilt and remorse because of how you made them feel. Chances are they will never return because you made them feel so bad. (7b)

If you are a salesperson, or ambitious in life to get ahead, don't climb the ladder at the cost of others. Learn how to use Persuasion instead of Manipulation. Assess your own intentions and make sure you are not misleading others for your own goals. For most of us, we would prefer not to walk all over someone else. There are some though that would have no cares of such selfish intent.

What then would you gain if you persuaded rather than manipulated?

Dr. Jason Jones, Psychologist and Executive Coach in Human Behaviour, outlines the positives of what you might gain:

- The satisfaction of using honesty.
- Such honesty may build up better connections. If some dislike your honesty, then turn your back on them. Walk away from those who prefer the art of manipulation.
- You will be a happier person with your life. Your achievements are genuine and not based on misleading clients, customers, friends and loved ones.

If you are in a position of leading others, such as a teacher, manager or parent, you will gain far more credibility by leading with care and compassion. Care, as in empathy; Compassion, as in taking into account other people's emotions. The darker ways can only lead to mistrust, broken relationships and failure, as others see you for what you truly are. (7c)

- For your own personal morality, do you want to stoop so low that you have no self-respect?
- For most of us, the answer is no.

The best and only way to deal with a manipulator is to say "NO."

- Stand up to them firmly but without confrontation.
- Let them know they can push all they want, but you will not weaken.
- Keep your own emotions hidden when you confront such a controlling bully.
- They will push you and you will tremble.

Your enemy will move on from you because you do not fuel their motives.

9. Conclusion

Time to take a deep breath and assimilate all the information presented to you, in this book.

If you are experiencing a stressful time, it can be useful to learn relaxation techniques. They will help you manage your mental wellbeing. Many of these can be done in the privacy of your own home, or even in a work situation.

Your mental wellbeing is as important as your physical health. It plays an important role in your happiness. You owe it to yourself to break out of any unhealthy stronghold that others might place on you, such as a manipulative character. No one could be happy living or working alongside another person who belittles them. Most particularly if that person coerces them into doing something they don't want to do. That is exactly what living with a controlling person is like, at work or home. You will feel trapped as they slowly destroy your self-esteem. If your partner or work colleague is never open to compromise, then they may well be manipulative and controlling. A healthy relationship, be it personal or work related, should be one whereby everyone feels comfortable.

Most of us grow up to be taught the social rules of good manners and acceptable behavior. Unfortunately, some either ignore this learning process or have no one to teach and guide them. We need positive role models in our informative years. Those who may have suffered abuse either physically or mentally as children, will be scarred in some form or another. Many will still manage a normal life, but it's unlikely that anyone can come out of a bad childhood unscathed.

Many of us struggle on in our daily lives. We perform routine tasks to make our lives pleasant and our loved ones happy. There comes a time when we do not always have the energy or inclination to help other people. Most of us will do a kindness along the way. Always though, our priorities are for our own loved ones. There is a certain necessity to be strong if you wish to make something of your life. Otherwise, depression can set in and you may drown in the many temptations around you. Excessive eating, or even worse the temptations of alcohol and drugs could seem an easy way out.

It does take courage to stand up to a controlling manipulative character, but you must be brave and see it through. Push them away from your life and keep them at arm's length. Don't be taken in by their false promises. If someone encompasses you so tightly that you feel you cannot breathe, then you must escape. A healthy relationship should not feel like that.

This book should enlighten you on how to cope with some of the problems you may face in life. It is meant only as a guide on how to deal with controlling manipulative relationships. It cannot give you your freedom. Only courage can do that. Build up your self-confidence. Take care of your health. For the sake of living a happy life, learn how to handle such controlling characters that may pass you by.

10. References

2a) <u>Greenwald, washington.edu pdf</u>

2b) <u>R. E. Petty, 1977 Study</u>

2c) <u>Burger 2009.pdf</u>

2d) <u>McCornack et al. (1992) Study</u>

2e) <u>Skinner Behaviorism</u>

2f) <u>Nudge Theory</u>

2g) <u>PsychologyToday.com</u>

2h) <u>Dr G Simon Texas University</u>

2i) <u>Wikipedia/Gaslighting</u>

3a) <u>Conversational Hypnosis</u>

3b) <u>Neuro-Linguistic Programming</u>

4a<u>) Pinker and Bloom semanticscholar.org</u>

4b)<u> K Harding The Diagnosis of Exclusion</u>

5a) <u>BOGOF tactic</u>

5b) <u>Daily Advertising Exposure</u>

5c) <u>Coworker Techniques to victimize</u>

5d) <u>Signs of a Control Freak</u>

THE ART OF READING PEOPLE

How To Analyze People Like The FBI

By

Richard Martinez

11. Introduction

This book is meant to remove or at least dampen one of the borders between people, perhaps the most problematic border – the fear of unknown.

You know this feeling when you suddenly have to understand the people you have nothing in common with? For instance, you've got a raise, and now you're a manager. The pay is definitely worth it, except now there are people you are responsible for, the people you're supposed to care for and understand on the deepest level possible – and you consider yourself an introvert in certain situations, maybe even awkward at times, not really into talking to unfamiliar folks, not very interested in what happens in their impenetrable heads and personal spaces . . . what to do?

Or maybe you have to work in sales, and you know how to sell: it must be their thing you're pitching to the client, not yours . . . but how do you know *what* their thing is?

Could be you're invested in this topic deeply: could be you're studying public relations, journalism, sociology, or any other profession which involves what we call *a keen eye for human character* – or you merely want to feel more comfortable around the opposite gender.

This book will be useful to you in every case mentioned above, and a million more unique cases we cannot even think of now.

This is because this book is a tool – something to be applied the way you desire, to a situation inherent to your own surroundings.

This book is devoted to the analysis of observed human behavior in interaction with another human (you or someone else) or without. This book will not make a Sherlock Holmes out of you – this fictional character's skills are supernatural – but it will, if applied properly, make you much more observant, attentive to others, and – in case you want it – more influential in situations where judgment of human character is involved.

So how do we know you are usually open to new people, but feel introverted in certain situations?

How do we know you have a great need for love and admiration but you rarely show it?

How do we know you'd rather give orders than take them?

This book will definitely help you to find this out.

The analysis of people, how does it really work? Let's start by saying the process is extremely individual, so basically the analysis of people is a multitude of analyses of different persons. And this is certainly an art, which makes it possible to fake analytical skills somewhat, and pretend to be the specialist in it while staying rather unskilled. On the other hand, also because it's an art, you can perfect your analytical skills for the entire life, and pick targets matching your experience, being able to map and grasp the most complex and hard characters.

We hope very much you're going to use the things you will learn for proper causes. Many people who are supposed to be good judges of character – businessmen, HR specialists, journalists, project managers and top managers – in fact don't possess the required knowledge, or are unable to apply it. Many people call themselves "empaths", and yet distance from unpleasant feelings, or strong feelings, and don't connect with people around them all too well, preferring isolation.

Some people employ analytical tricks and techniques just to use the obtained knowledge for manipulation or exploitation of others.

This book is to teach you how you can feel what other people feel, the real empathy, something very simple to explain yet very hard to master for one simple reason: we're often not ready to fully embrace the perspective of another human being, share and understand their pain, breathe in their personal life and see what drives them. This book will talk a lot about remaining objective, restrained, and properly distanced as you judge another person's posture, actions, voice timbre, and so on – just because otherwise your own influence, your own emotional interference will bar you from proper judgment. The book's ultimate goal is, however, not to make you into a cold and calculative character akin to Niccolò Machiavelli – in contrary, we will try to explain why such behavior is counterproductive and gains you nothing.

This book's ultimate goal is to make you more open and more confident in your social and business communications on a personal level, able to know people, and apply the obtained knowledge in a meaningful way.

This book's goal is to teach you to think carefully before you act, and be kind to others in your choices and actions.

This book unifies the working knowledge of a few people, including a top manager, a UX/monetization expert, a behaviorist, and a free-time journalist. The experience described in this book is purely personal, yet the knowledge is practical, based on existing, and named, studies and research projects. The practical part of the knowledge found in this book is meant to be applied to any sort of situation, from a business meeting to a romantic date.

Yet first of all, this book is written to be brief and handy. So let us move on!

12. The Ethnics of Communication

The analysis of people is not a passive skill. It's not some kind of a special burst of attention that could be activated at will, after which it automatically tells you things about people around you, Sherlock Holmes way. The analysis of people implies normal observation, not supernatural zoom-in slow motion injections of private knowledge. The more attentive you are to people around you, the better you'll be able to analyze them, but this attention doesn't mean perfect vision and superhuman insight, this attention is more of what Bill Murray's character does by the end of *The Groundhog Day* – this attention means caring about people around you, noticing what they do, and what happens to them.

And this is a very important point we have to start from: mindfulness and kindness towards people. After you practice the techniques described in this book, you will learn to know more about those you will interact with. You'll know what makes these people happy, and you'll know what makes them sad. Basically, you will know how these individuals react to different stimuli, what makes them tick.

You may be inclined to use this knowledge, this special understanding of people, to manipulate somebody, to exploit someone's weak spots, to overpower their insufficient will with yours, or cause harm to them. After you read this book, you'll know that human conscience, the knowledge of rights and wrongs, is merely a social instinct telling you whether you'll be accepted and loved by your own kind for every consecutive word you speak and action you take. Like many instincts, this one could be dampened or even overridden with reason and rationalization. Many people do harm to others consciously with no morals to stop them, just 2 because they know this will go unpunished, or is somehow sanctioned or allowed, or even generally approved of amongst their peers.

So in fact it's not your conscience that must stop you from using this book's methods for a wrong cause, but your honor, your knowledge of yourself as a decent, trustworthy, and caring person. Let's just finish by saying we're all adult people, and deep inside we all know right from wrong, merely by knowing how we wouldn't like to be treated ourselves; so the caution line is there, and it's visible at all times.

In this book, we will, as Sherlock Holmes would, put cold reason in the first place, and brush emotions aside. We will talk about the dangers of compassion as something undesired, distorting your worldview. We will praise logic a lot, and it may seem we talk about matters of the heart as if they are something lowly and primitive. This is not so.

Analysis of people is a research, it demands objectivity, it relies on logic and reason, so naturally, it is a task best done with a cool head on one's shoulders. Still, while applying the knowledge, always remember to consult with your heart first. May your deeds be as pleasant to those around you as they are pleasant to you.

We're all social beings after all, and cold analytical people are little fun. Just so those you interact with feel comfortable, never allow the methods we describe in this book overrule your normal human communication. Even more so, some of the techniques we describe will work better if your subject feels love from your side, or at least is unaware of your cold analytical activities, if they're going on in the background. Your correspondent being relaxed and feeling warmth from your side is always beneficial to you.

And always remember – by studying others, we know more and more about our own selves.

13. Human Character

Imagine a monkey carrying a computer. The computer is able to look around, think, analyze, and talk, yet is completely unable to move on its own. The monkey is free to run around, sometimes even where the computer points it to. And yet, ultimately it's the monkey who decides where to go, according to its feelings.

This is exactly how human consciousness works.

On the most basic levels of cognition, or, poetically speaking, deep inside – we are all wild animals, primates obeying certain primal urges and drives. Our basic behavior is instinctive – you know that feeling when you travel to work early in the morning "riding on autopilot" and only really wake up on arriving there? Or, how you become bored of *Tetris* because you start playing it without really thinking? This learned behavior all belongs to our primal core, our monkey carrying around our reason, the computer, which could be preoccupied with something totally different while the primate is riding a subway playing a primate-oriented mobile game.

Reason is defined very directly. Reason is the part of us that speaks. It's the part of us that either talks or converses within us. Reason defines where our attention and active imagination are currently directed, so while the primate is playing its mobile game, the computer may be actively analyzing someone of opposite sex sitting across.

Sometimes the monkey and the computer argue. Think of how a person trying to quit smoking feels. Their reason demands certain things, while their primal being may respond with an entire tantrum to get its point across, and who knows who will win in the end!

The trick is, the "you", the thinking part of you, associates itself with the talking part, the reason. And the reason is always happy to explain things away. Which is why, even if your choice and the actions that followed it were instinctive, done on autopilot, in response to some primal urge, your reason will still claim responsibility for them, and rationalize anything you chose and done in the past, then explain to you why such choices were made, based on logic. It will be done in retrospective, in hindsight, yet fed to you as something that truly and certainly happened before you acted, not after.

It's really important to differentiate between the things one does automatically, acting on a whim, without thinking slowly and attentively prior to it – and the things done consciously, after a true consideration, which would involve the revision of all possible outcomes, weighing them against each other, etc.

In his book *Thinking, Fast and Slow,* Daniel Kahneman discusses two modes of thinking – fast and slow thinking, as you might have guessed. This is exactly it. Our monkey thinks fast, it basically always knows what it wants and how do get it. It only turns to the computer it carries around when it doesn't know what to do, when it needs something difficult dealt with, things calculated, slowly and carefully – the way the computer does it.

So this is what you absolutely have to remember when approaching another person from the analytical standpoint: you're dealing with a dualistic being, the reason of which may work in two modes: either doing its job, or emulating it, letting the basic urges and drives pull its owner around, and then explaining to them why it was the most logical thing to do. Always try and observe in which mode the person of your interest is functioning at the moment: the reason mode, or the body mode? (Since primal urges are normally born of the body.)

This is where some religions find its concept of sin: their followers are basically required to always put their reason first, and suppress the cravings of their body. What happens if the computer tries to fight the monkey and subdue it? Results vary, but we can certainly tell such behavior is destructive.

Does a human being possess a freedom of will? This question is rather philosophical – is there multiple choice, or is the Universe linear, every state of it predetermined by the state that came before? We cannot know. What we can know reviewing every decision taken by us or someone else we analyze is, was reason involved in making it, or were feelings, "the heart" involved?

In practice, if a decision was taken more or less instantly, it will be an unconscious "lizard mind" decision, the choice our monkey made without consulting with the computer.

And if we look into our own daily choices, we'll see in 98% of the cases the monkey-made choice was indeed mundane, very typical, repetitive – perhaps inherent to this particular place and/or time. We know our monkey is trained to carry out this part of our daily routine, so we gladly entrust our actions to this "autopilot", and keep our reason preoccupied with something else.

But this also means our actions become more direct, simple, and predictable; our monkey is after all but an animal following a simple pattern of well-learned repetitive behaviors: brush teeth, wash face, use towel, go to kitchen, put kettle on. If there's suddenly an accident at this point, something's on fire or falls on the floor and smashes, then we're suddenly "back on earth" – the computer switches back from its screensaver showing distant lands, and quickly runs the analysis routine: what must be done? What to take care of first? At the same time, the monkey holding it may panic, and then the computer's attention will be switched to pacifying the panicking animal, taking control of it.

In any case, after the danger is gone, we suddenly feel more alive, more present in the moment. This happens because our body and mind both entered the mode of behavior we shall call an "alert" mode. This happens when our reason, our active attention, is concentrated on here and now, the beautiful moment of full self-awareness, full internal agreement, when as much of ourselves is under our control as possible. This is when we become lethal, war-ready, and totally unpredictable for an observer. What actually happens is, our reason, our common sense, takes the full hold, and the animal is happy to follow it into the fray.

To better imagine the two modes of action, the "autopilot" mode and the "alert" mode, we could turn to literary fiction: in *Strange Case of Dr. Jekyll and Mr. Hyde*, the protagonist finds a way to split his character into two segregated beings, one fully driven by instinct; violent, destructive, and asocial(sic!) Mr. Hyde; another a young doctor driven purely by reason – kind, clever, and righteous. It's curious to see the dualism of human consciousness presented this way back in the XIX century, back when primal, animalistic urges and passions in human being were considered sinful and shameful in society, and incredible restraint was practiced in social communication: you could only interact with another human being through a complex prism of etiquette, which called for your attention and involved long and complex actions, and speeches thoughtfully prepared, nothing ever rushed.

Then comes XX century, and Sigmund Freud, who calls the primal animalistic part "id", and the exalted being of pure reason "super-ego" (our ego, then, is like a slider of self-identification running back and forth between the two ends of this persona spectrum. Id still sounds a bit sinful, a Mr. Hyde of sorts. The soon-emerging school of Jungians calls the same thing a "Shadow self", and yet again, it sounds like something evil.

These were perceptions of specific times.

In our day and age, "staying true to oneself", "listening to one's heart", "following one's inner calling" and such being looked favorably on – seems like our inner, primal urges and drives were finally legalized, and in this light, we see Mr. Hyde is not really a monster – it's more of a poet torn apart by corporal desires, a being which represents our internal warmth, the love we carry inside – the qualities a cold creature of pure empty reason, the supposedly righteous and sociable Dr. Jekyll, doesn't really possess. People who rely on reason alone, and follow their personal gains while brushing emotions away, we consider heartless, cruel, cold, Machiavellian, and so on. Ritualistic conversations and pretense are no longer norms of society.

Seems like in our day and age, we finally see the key to personal happiness: the balance of both modes of action, a regular person staying in the middle of the spectrum instead of swinging wildly between the two absolutes, something XIX century's society was famous for.

Still, remember this while analyzing someone: in the "alert" reasonable mode, people act differently from their "autopilot" instinctive mode. Expect to see less patterned behavior when the person's reason is actively involved, or expect deviations from the observed pattern of behavior at any moment.

We discuss patterns of behavior in greater detail in the next chapter.

14. Masks People Wear

All the world's a stage, William Shakespeare said, *and all the men and women merely players; They have their exits and their entrances, and one man in his time plays many parts.*

This is of course true; and even when one individual acts as a different person in front of different people, it doesn't necessarily mean duplicity or pretense, or even an act. Your boss (or client, if you are a freelancer) is one person in front of you and another in front of their children, and this difference of behavior and appearance is a social norm.

It so happens we do wear masks, and many of us have to change their mask twice or even thrice a day – just to put bread on our table – and we don't even call ourselves actors!

Because it's basic survival.

And this is something quite important to remember: basic survival instincts predate everything in a person. They are the primary directives, the ultimate priority calls of the wild. There's a popular book by Eric Berne call *Games People Play* (this is a recommended read, as we even named our chapter in accordance with it) which talks a lot about role models, the patterns of behavior we love seeing in others – sometimes in a favorite cartoon character! – which we then copy and think of as inherent to our own unique, authentic selves.

One thing is definitely true: each personality is built upon this primal, absolutely wild, fight-or-flight creature buried inside each of us, the creature we become when we hit rock bottom, when we are reduced to our lowest, and our survival becomes the only thing we care about. Think werewolves.

Now imagine someone who, instead of a wolf, becomes a Chihuahua scared of its own shadow. And this someone, who remains quiet and careful while at the brink, may turn out to have a much higher survival potential. You never know how someone's survival mode persona looks until you find yourselves together between a rock and a hard place, hence a wise observation of old: *homo homini lupus est,* which is again, the *werewolf* theme, the *Beware of Evil Mr. Hyde!* theme, which is not how it has to be, mind the Chihuahua!

A good manager or military commander takes mental notes of their team members' behaviors during a crisis, pretty much like a captain would take their team through at least one storm prior to real adventures, because this "panic mode" personality is what you want to know about a person you entrust certain things with.

Post-apocalyptic and survivor movies and books often display people driven to the brink suddenly becoming paranoid, randomly aggressive, selfish, escapist, and so on – but mostly the theme remains the same: as if a thin veil of civilization was swept away by this catastrophe or another, and you behold a human being's terrible true face, and it's a snarling grimace of a cavemen, or an animal of even more basic kind.

So this book of Eric Berne, the one we highly recommend, *Games People Play* – finds an interesting application when we are speaking of this borderline character, the animalistic side exposed, the Mr. or Ms. Hyde pole of the personality spectrum of a given human being.

If you ever read fables and think about the masks people wear, then you'll remember what the art of fable is all about: a fable is a human social situation played out on animals. And this is a very interesting observation, for indeed, this "survival mode" will often manifest as behavior resembling that of some animal: in a crisis situation, the person may jump at people and roar like a lion, or retract into a shell like a mollusk, etc.

Another strange yet beautiful application of the role model idea of Eric Berne: for human beings, especially speaking of cultural symbolism, it's very natural to mimic certain behavior of animals, or, say, cartoon characters they liked as little kids. We primates are great mimics, and, finding ourselves amidst the wild we will often unconsciously put on a mask of whatever crazy thing we think represents our true character best. This is the factor that could make horoscopes relevant – never ignore a person's Zodiac sign if the person in question *believes* in Zodiac signs!

When everything is quiet and boring though, when our inner animals are well-fed and fluffy – this is when they turn back human. And the faces of humanity are . . . yet again, according to Eric Berne, Erich Fromm, Irwin Yalom – the faces of humanity are shaped and molded by cultures through fairytales and visions of our childhood. Little kids watch life in all its many facets; they pick their role models from the heroic, epic characters of their childhood, and create their first romantic ideals. Will these ideals stand the test of time, or will this childish personality be swept away and replaced by a more practical mindset, picked up from books and movies for adults, or live role models of adulthood? Or, perhaps, the character of this child will be reborn in the streets, in the concrete jungle, each mutation of it a dose of harsh street wisdom?

In any case, through simple and direct social lessons, both lived through and seen/read about somewhere – the entity we call a human character, or a personality, is born, and by now we see sometimes this personality has more than a single side. Our society is still happy to present a single person with many roles that may require a totally different character, so we normally only become the true ourselves when driven to the brink. Only forced into the game of survival – or into any other primal activity, like a sexual act – the human being dons all masks and becomes a singular creature driven by basic instincts. We may safely state one may never truly know a person until this part of their personality is revealed, observed, and known.

And the truth must be said: the multitude of masks people otherwise wear is endless, and fluidity of them is extreme. This is because all higher level habits, so-called "social instincts" – they are learned instincts, and learned things could be unlearned in a wink of an eye. Someone may eat bread all their life, then hear about glutens and quit gluten products forever, which leads them to change their entire lifestyle, which ultimately turns them into another person, someone their relatives hardly even recognize – and it happens as easy as that, a small article on glutens.

All because learned habits are so easy to unlearn. Habits are easy to change. People tend to revise their life once in a while. Some of them do it every morning. You never know.

What we have to remember is, no matter how many masks the big carnival of society may force upon us, one part, this "rock bottom" part, always remains true to itself, hence the proverb: *A friend in need is a friend indeed.*

15. Empathy and Compassion

We all know what compassion is – it's a feeling of mutual care and attention found in mammals and birds but not found in many reptiles, for instance, found in rattlesnakes but not in tortoises or lizards.

Compassion is something we need to develop to become a good person to be around: it's your mindfulness of other people's wishes and needs, responsiveness to them (for compassion doesn't make sense when it doesn't involve action on one's part).

For the purposes of analysis, compassion is harmful.

You remember how Sherlock Holmes is normally portrayed – a rather cold and restrained character, even ready to risk the lives of the people he is supposed to care for in order to prove some theory

of his? And it's not like Sherlock is a bad person –
he can do little about this feature of his character, as
it's only a side effect of his "deductive method", or
rather, the reverse, dark side of his highly observant
and analytical mindset. It's merely the nature of the
game: a good analyst stays out of the picture to
preserve it from their own interference, or at least
limit this interference to the actions dictated by logic:
*the criminal must be stopped, who cares if a young
widow suffers from a PTSD as a result!*

This doesn't mean, however, that people analysis
doesn't involve empathy. Quite the opposite: this
analysis is *based* on empathy, or at least on
something called "cognitive" or "cold empathy",
merely because a compassionate detective sobbing
and hugging the victim is of no use to anybody.

Let's refer to Wikipedia:

Affective empathy, also called emotional empathy:
the capacity to respond with an appropriate emotion

to another's mental states. Our ability to empathize emotionally is based on emotional contagion: being affected by another's emotional or arousal state.

Cognitive empathy: the capacity to understand another's perspective or mental state. The terms cognitive empathy and theory of mind or mentalizing are often used synonymously, but due to a lack of studies comparing theory of mind with types of empathy, it is unclear whether these are equivalent.

"Mentalizing" is exactly what we need; it's the concept that implies people analysis, detective work. It means the kind of insight into another human being that doesn't sway you emotionally. And these modes, affective empathizing and cognitive empathizing, are so different we could even claim they are mutually exclusive, or at least affection is something you want to restrain from while analyzing people, because the saying *love is blind* is very true, same as *blind rage* is.

How does it work? Imagine seeing a charity worker asking for money, carrying a sign with a picture of a traumatized child. Your affective empathy tells you: *it's terrible, to be this child. The life of this poor baby is sheer torture. It's horrible, what happened to this poor little thing. And this charity worker, such a noble person, doing such a righteous job!* And so, your compassion pushes your hand toward your wallet.

Cognitive empathy keeps you clear of these powerful feelings though. Yes, this child must have felt terrible when they photographed it. Yet the logic protests. How do we know who took this picture? And when? Is this child related to the money in the charity worker's box somehow? Is this charity worker a real deal, or is it a con artist who uses shock imagery to trigger people into donating money? This is something cold empathy is about, looking to understand another person's motives without being carried away by emotions.

Empathy has nothing do to with *sympathy,* although they are often being confused, and you see people who like to imagine themselves in place of someone else calling themselves *empaths,* although this is an absolutely wrong, inverted understanding of empathy. "Walking in someone else's shoes", imagining ourselves in the position of another person, is called *sympathy.* It normally resolves in us saying things like: "Don't worry, it happened to me a lot, it's fine", or "In your place, I'd go and see a doctor immediately." This way, we learn nothing about another human being, because we sympathize, not empathize with them.

Empathy is your ability to put aside your own self, your own worldview, experience, your own *angle,* and accept the world of this another human being, truly understand what moves them. How do we know if we truly understand another person? Easy! Remember how they say *lovers and fools think alike?* It happens exactly because lovers and *fools* empathize with each other easily, open up to each other the way their thoughts, feelings, and actions become synchronized to a degree they exclaim the same phrase in a certain situation.

Empathy is your ability to become another person and replace your own world with someone else's. It's like playing someone else on stage – except the stage is your imagination. How well can you empathize with me? 100% empathy means you can predict my words and actions perfectly.

Remember how a detective retraces the criminal's steps through the scene of the crime, touching something, pretending to drop something? This is about how his or her empathizing with the criminal would look – except of course there's no absolute need to move around in precise motions of the criminal, just getting into the criminal's mood and looking around the room would be enough.

Before you can do it in your head though, a good idea would be to practice it physically, learning *the dance* and its moves.

Cognitive empathy becomes possible because of mirror neurons: the part of our brain responsible for learning new behaviors through observation of another human beings (or higher animals), no matter if we observe them physically or review conscious mental images of them. We watch how it's done, we try to do it ourselves (mentally or physically), we fake it till we make it, and sooner or later we learn how it's done (creating new neuron connections) or abandon hope (and let the whole thing fade away). If you look carefully into this learning process, you'll see it looks very close to how cognitive empathy works: *copying and striving for a perfect match. Lovers and fools think alike.*

This is why, in order to analyze a human being in front of us, we must learn to switch to their viewpoint. It means we must learn to *copy* them, to *become* them, to *think* like them, and this is not a pulp fiction cliché!

To know one's enemy, one must think like their enemy – Sun Tzu, "The Art of War", a very ancient book.

In order to catch a criminal, any police detective will tell you, *you need to think like a criminal.*

16. Muscular Core, Posture and Breathing

The first thing we keep an eye for in a person is the condition of their muscles. Is the person tense or relaxed? How high the tension is and where is it concentrated? Is it a prelude to a fight or a flight?

The best way to find out is to copy your subject's muscular core state, just look at how their muscles are arranged and try to arrange yours the same way. There's a good expression, "to carry oneself", and your goal will be to carry yourself just as them. Your copy doesn't have to be identical, just close enough so you feel close enough to themselves – imitate them as close to perfection as your present acting skills allow (to be a good judge of character, a good analyst, you don't have to be a good actor, but it helps – remember Sherlock Holmes and his transformations?) It isn't hard – just contract whatever they have contracted and keep it that way!

Now, as we learned to carry ourselves like our
subject of study, we must learn to walk like them
and breathe like them, or at least pretend to do it,
deep inside.

Much can be learned from a human posture and
walk: people with bad eyesight recognize and spot
their relatives and friends by their silhouette, their
posture, their walk in the crowd of hundreds of
people, alone, as easy as a person with keen
eyesight would. Can you stand or sit exactly as your
subject does, and feel as comfortable as they
seem? Can you breathe like them, at the same rate,
with the same depth, following the same intervals?

Try and practice it alone at first, looking at a video of
someone else. Soon you'll be able to perform it
mentally, running the process almost completely in
your imagination. As soon as your musculature and
posture *imprint* will feel identical to that of your
subject; as soon as your combined breath sounds

like one, it's time to analyze their non-verbal message.

Are they demonstrating the will to move closer, shorten the distance between you – or are they trying to distance themselves from you? Is their posture open towards you (face, chest, and groin unobstructed by limbs) or closed from you? (Folded arms, crossed knees, etc.) If their posture is closed, don't jump to conclusions: they may position themselves this way merely for comfort, not because they'd like to lock themselves away from you. If your object's posture is closed and is comfortable – they are likely an introvert. With extroverts, expect abrupt changes in posture, quick movements ahead (lean towards the person they're speaking to, or reach for them), meant to shorten the distance between them.

Body language is a nation-specific feature of communication – in some countries it's hardly used, while in the others two conversing people may resemble two windmills. Still, you can normally detect the heat of discussion by the amount and smoothness of gesturing, even when watching the speakers from the distance. The rougher, sharper gestures become, the less controlled they are, the higher the likeness of a conflict.

A conflict is something often provoked by the opposition, or a third party, with intent to unsettle us, upset us, or make us lose our temper and act out. Our goal in this situation will be to retain control of ourselves. This doesn't mean suppressing our anger or bottling our frustration. This means dissolving the heat of emotions in the cold presence of our reason. This means starting with controlled breathing, restrained posture, and slow relaxation of the muscle core, resetting it to absolute calm.

A person in control is not someone gritting their teeth, holding reins back – it's the person showing calm restraint and conscious choice of their words and actions. Remember the monkey and the computer? The last one is the analyst; the first one lives for battle, and spots a good fight miles away. There's a good use for this quality too: your instincts will tell you when the situation is about to heat up a bit too much, so your reason could be there in time to prevent unnecessary drama before it has a chance to happen!

The point is neither of the two parts of one's consciousness must be restrained or removed from the interaction. When the reason is cast aside, no civilized communication is possible: any conversation will quickly derail and devolve into something childish, silly, and virtually useless for any purposes but socializing itself. If the emotional part is suppressed, the person starts feeling discomfort.

This is a very important point, and it happens to be twofold: whenever you spot manifestations of discomfort in either yourself or your object, you will know it happens because the primal part, the emotional part, is subdued by reason. This may happen when the person's reason doesn't want to give something away, yet their body – heartbeat, breathing, perspiration – seems eager to betray them, so they try and shut it off using reason, forcing themselves under control for a period of time, after which their animalistic part will inevitably act out. You must have seen how, leaving the room after a difficult meeting, people will be overly childish and agitated, exclaiming loudly, pushing each other, craving some sort of physical gratification – it's all the backlash of self-control imposed by reason, now lifted.

Hence, to stay comfortable, to remain in full control of oneself – which is something you want to practice in order to become a good restrained analyst – one must never suppress their inner feelings! It's hard to give advice on how your computer could keep your monkey in check, as this is a personal thing, inherent to your own character. There's a huge number of venting and confidence-building techniques out there, and you're free to try them all! Just remember this simple rule: by indulging a certain whim of your animal, you grow it, not reduce it. For instance, aggressive behavior does not deplete aggression, in contrary, it increases your aggressiveness – same as being afraid will not deplete your fear.

Still, there *are* techniques helping you to drop the level of aggression and overcome fear, from the most basic things like counting to ten, naming objects around you mentally, or drinking a glass of water – down to counseling and transcendental meditation. In this book, we'll merely say the solution is out there, and self-control is essential if you want to stay an involved yet unbiased party.

On the other hand, this is what you want to notice in the behavior of your subject: not their controlled, reasonable actions, but their slips, their subliminal telltales; the small movements, expressions, and changes in posture that happen without the subject noticing. How to interpret this body language? The problem is, it's not only inherent to a particular culture, but also varies from one individual to another.

Many sources claim they're able to teach you some kind of universal list of telltales, enabling you to tell truth from lies, present you with recipes of telling an act from the real deal – but these sources are at best-generalized information, sometimes applicable to many people, enough to make it seem true, but definitely not to be applied to just everyone. The truth is, only your own experience, attentiveness, and insight will help you to read another person's body language, for there are as many body languages as there are different people.

For instance, when someone is trying to touch or hide a part of their face – lips, the nose, an ear – it's normally considered a sign of secretiveness, the telltale of a person lying or trying to hide some information from the listener. In many cases it's indeed so – and still, be careful not to call someone a liar just because they tend to rub their three-day stubble while they're thinking.

Another popular facial feature to be pointed out as a telltale: a genuine smile would cause crinkles around eyes, while a fake smile normally wouldn't. Yet again, in many cases it may be true – we often hear about "someone smiling while their eyes remain cold". Then again, the experiments show the "smiling eyes" can be faked more or less easily, and if you were to encounter a sociopathic person, someone good at mimicry – you'd never catch them faking a smile. (We'll talk about spotting such individuals in Chapter 8.)

Approach tendencies in the posture of your subject may mean aggression – or they could mean affection, and only your judgment may discern between the two. If your subject demonstrates avoidance tendencies – this, yet again, could mean an entire spectrum of emotions: apathy, fear, disgust, mistrust, submission, meekness, and so on.

A good analyst would always view the non-verbal signals of their subject as a part of the bigger picture, applying to them the knowledge of this person as a whole. Even a habit as simple as biting one's fingernails – are you sure I bite mine when I'm nervous? It may happen a person tends to stick their thumb in their mouth while they're thoughtful, relaxed, their attention directed inward – miles from feeling nervous!

Always remember: what you see is only half of the picture. Another half, no less important, is what you hear.

17. The Heat of Conversation

Spoken language is an extremely powerful tool. Ants, bees, and birds may be far better builders than us humans, and a simple flower could be more beautiful than an artwork of a genius painter, and still, it's the ability to formulate our thoughts in words that set us apart from the rest of nature. Thanks to spoken language, we human beings may by right call ourselves the only creatures on Earth able not only to collect information, but also to store it, organize it, and pass it on to other humans. Words are powerful, and they certainly could kill.

And still, before we even concern ourselves with them and their meaning, we're going to listen for something else, something we could do before we could even speak. A poet could have called it the *songs people sing.*

Picture a two-year-old child, not yet able to speak a single word. Still, it's able to get its point across by the intonation only! All it can do is hum and moan, and yet, our child is capable of humming and moaning in a hundred different ways, and many of its intonations are so universal and primordial, we don't need the child's mother to interpret for us – in 99% of cases, we are able to tell what the child wants to say just because we can, because the baby cooing language is pretty much universal!

Ask any professional negotiator, be it a diplomat, a manager, an HR, or a salesperson – while waiting for the other party to respond, what exactly they anticipate the most, where their attention is concentrated? You'll hear a unanimous "it's not *what* they say – it's *how* they say it".

Remember how the most basic, primal part of the human character always acts first? By listening to intonation, we hear the voice of this very part of the speaker, their instinctive side. What matters here first is emotional involvement: how short are the pauses before your subject's answers? If your subject responds to verbal remarks addressed to them almost immediately, taking no time to employ reason, you can be sure their feelings are very much involved. Expect the answers of your subject to be passionate, biased, and loaded with emotion. In this state, a person tends to say things they wouldn't part with otherwise – be sure not to miss anything important from the information being delivered!

If pauses before their answers are long, this could happen for two reasons: either your subject's answers are less emotional, well-prepared, tested and weighed mentally, and employ as much common sense (slow thinking) as possible – or your subject is unsure of what to say. Yet again, listen to the intonation and voice timbre to understand which case you are dealing with. Is the speaker's voice confident, solid, and flat – or is their intonation of a shaky, roaming, ever-changing kind? Imagine the air column inside the speaker's lungs – the physical volume of air inside their lungs and throat. Is it stable, well-measured, and carefully replenished by breathing, or is it unsteady and erratic, often making your subject hyperventilate or lose breath?

And yet again, speaking of interpretation of your findings – everything about a particular human being is personal, and every particular individual is, well, individual. Same as we don't recommend using pop-psychological "detective work" on your subject's posture, muscular core, and breathing – the same way, applying all kinds of generalized pigeon-hole labeling to your subject's intonations will inevitably cause fundamental errors in your judgment.

Yes, we could say if the speaker's intonation is weak, shaky, and rambling, it may speak of their uncertainty, lack of knowledge, perhaps even their weak attempt at lies! Except in some people, it's their normal voice timbre. When your subject takes a big pause and makes a thoughtful face – does it mean they're really thinking on what to say next, or it's just their concept of polite and intelligent conversation, during which they're *supposed* to act this way? Yet again, it's very individual.

Speaking of truth and lies, all you need to know to be able to discern one from another is, lying involves imagination, while telling truth only involves remembering. What does it tell us?

First of all, imagination involves some brain work, and if the person in question doesn't use their imagination professionally on regular basis – like an artist or a con man would do – then we definitely shall expect a longer pause before the answer is given, perhaps hear a change in voice timbre or spot minor changes in the facial expression. An inexperienced liar will also try to avoid eye contact, blush, or sweat excessively.

If the lie was prepackaged however, and the person practiced its delivery prior to the conversation, it could come so fast it's going to be *too* fast. If the expected answer was supposed to involve reason, slow thinking – and it came straight off, like something instinctive – there's a high chance the answer was prepackaged, and on closer examination the information provided may prove to be untrue.

Untrue – or just a mess, a jumble of fact and fiction, a biased rationalization, a bout of wishful thinking? How do we tell?

The only way we can tell is by listening carefully, memorizing our findings, learning more and more about this particular individual.

And this is a very important point. In the next chapter, we will review several active analytical techniques, something you can say or ask in a conversation to quickly find out important details about your subject's character. We will no longer remain a silent observer – and this is where danger lies!

Many of us love to talk. Many of us enjoy listening to ourselves in a conversation. Some of us tend to ignore the bulk of what was said by someone else, as our own pleasant and elegant phrasing, our own rhetorical prowess drowns out everything else. This is especially true for beginner psychologists (or people who read up on psychology): they are so sure of their own claims they even forget to match them against the actual individual they're talking to. Many of the books these people read provide them with easy answers: this one is an extrovert, this one an introvert. This person is a subtype 2 of type A, while this one is a subtype 1 of type B. It's so hard to listen and observe patiently when you can just make statements and point fingers instead!

And yet, all theoretical knowledge, no matter if false or true, is useless without the proper practical mindset. You can cover your subject with labels and categories from head to toes, and yet learn nothing about them. Or even worse, you can develop a whole wrong picture of them, backed up by tons of material you read, and even the practical, observed evidence will be unable to sway you from your firm yet wrong belief.

To make sure this won't happen, always remember: you are the analyst! Not the other person who wrote the book. Not the book itself. No matter how much you read, it's nothing but your own perception, your own knowledge of this particular individual that will tell you what's really going on inside their head. If the person in front of you is someone new, someone you hadn't studied well yet, no amount of theoretical knowledge will help you close the gap – only the practical observation and communication will ensure you know as much about your subject as it's possible to know.

What if you're bad at noticing things, easily distracted, not really observant? Let's just say it works like muscle! The analytical skill is not a superpower you will obtain on reading this book. It's something we discover in ourselves and develop! The more you practice analysis, the better at analysis you become, so make it a habit.

Whenever you're free, and there are many unfamiliar subjects in front of you, switch the scanning mode on! Try and figure out things about people around you. Whenever you're lost and don't know what to look at, use cognitive empathy. Tell yourself: I am this person now. Who am I? How do I feel? What am I going to do or say next? The better you're at this, the more confident you will feel about your predictions and the higher correlation of them and actual reality you will observe. Even better – by becoming more attentive to others, more eager to watch and listen, showing more interest in people around you, you will become much more pleasant company! We all like it when people notice our new haircut. When someone notices what's happening inside of us and offers their attention in response – it could be enough for us to fall in love.

Up to now, we were speaking about passive observation only. In the next chapter, we will finally discuss the active methods of analysis, the things you could say and do to find out more about somebody. But the fact remains: when the observer enters the picture, the picture will inevitably change. Only use the active methods if you cannot afford passive learning! Remember what Al Pacino said in his famous speech in *The Devil's Advocate?* "Free will, it's like butterfly wings – once touched, they never get off the ground."

Remember an old saying about how we've got two ears and one mouth, so we should listen twice and talk once? We'll go as far as tell you to *listen always and only talk when it's needed.*

18. Barnum Effect, Cold Reading, Mirroring

Let's say plain observation doesn't help anymore. It may happen we learned everything we could from our subject while observing them passively, and no new information may possibly be obtained. Or, could be our time is limited, and we need to get to know the subject quickly, in a matter of minutes. When this happens, we cannot afford to stay a passive observer – we have to act!

The worst thing you can do in this case is resort to interrogation. Be it a job interview, a TV show, or a romantic date – subjecting the person of your interest in a line of tedious pre-fabricated questions will bore them out really quickly. If you read the previous chapters carefully, and your observational habits are in place, then you'll notice after only a few questions your subject will become aloof, unwilling, demotivated, and so on. We all hate answering plain questions about our character, and when asked to "name 5 of your worst qualities" we can even get angry with the interviewer. *How is it even their business?* It's a very effective way to terminate your warm, humane relations with someone – to give them a blank to fill, bore them to tears, and then intrude into their personal space in such an aggressive manner.

Wouldn't it be better to open our active analysis with letting the person in question know we do understand them, can identify with them, see what they are and appreciate it? How do we open our conversation then, and what do we say to instantly break the ice and predispose the person towards us?

Here we must turn to trick fortune tellers and mediums use; the trick that may give you a hint why horoscopes and Tarot readings seem to work although they don't make sense scientifically.

This trick is called a *Barnum effect,* also known as *Forer effect,* named either in honor of a famous showman Phineas Barnum, the first registered user of so-called "Barnum statements", which he employed in order to "telepathically read" his audience members – or after an American psychologist Bertram Forer, who analyzed the psychological mechanisms behind said "telepathy" and recreated the situation experimentally. What he did was offer each of his students a "unique personality evaluation chart" consisting entirely of the statements which seem personal, yet in fact apply to pretty much anyone. The students were asked to evaluate the accuracy of every statement as applied to their character – and the correlation points were incredibly high, *4.7 out of 5* being the median, despite the fact every student received exactly the same set of statements, for instance:

- *You have a tendency to be critical of yourself;*

- *Some of your aspirations tend to be pretty unrealistic;*

- At times you are extroverted, affable, sociable, while at other times you are introverted, wary, reserved;

- While you have some personality weaknesses, you are generally able to compensate for them, etc.

Said Barnum effect is a perfect initial step in a conversation during which you intend to obtain close knowledge of your subject. Remember those personal questions from our introduction?

How do we know you are usually open to new people, but feel introverted in certain situations?

We know it because it applies to pretty much everyone. Doesn't it?

How do we know you have a great need for love and admiration but you rarely show it?

Same thing. Isn't it?

How do we know you'd rather give orders than take them?

This one is tricky; of course some people lack initiative, and they'd rather take orders and worry about nothing . . . the question is, would such a person be reading a book on analysis of people? And the sure bet is, no, they wouldn't.

One of the reasons why the Barnum effect works, besides the generalized statements, is something called a *confirmation bias*. It claims we tend to agree with descriptions of our character *if we like them*, not because of them being true. Maybe you do show a need for admiration – you could be needy and even narcissistic for all we know! – and yet, who would disagree with someone calling them reserved, confident, a strong and silent type? It takes certain courage and objectivity, disagreeing with a good thing said about ourselves – so normally, we tend to agree.

Where is the analysis though? What we were speaking about until now is related to establishing contact, breaking the ice. Of what use to us is someone's "yes" said in response to a Barnum statement?

The analysis begins when we continue the discourse and narrow things down; zoom in on certain qualities of the subject's character that interest us. This technique is called *cold reading* ("cold" means you're honestly unfamiliar with your subject) and it's employed equally often by salesmen, show businessmen, journalists, and con artists.

It helps you study your subject while pretending to know them well from the start. This way, the conversation is much warmer. In fact you can regulate the warmth by interchanging ego-pleasing confirmation-biased remarks, then offering critical judgment in a reasonable and "sobering" manner, finding out actual new information about the subject. Let's see how Susan interviews Mark for the job.

Susan: "Please tell me how high your skill level is."

Mark: "I'm a senior specialist."

Susan: "Do you know Python? And C++?"

Mark: "Yes, I do, I'm familiar with both."

Susan: "Are you also familiar with MySQL?"

Mark: "Yes."

Susan: "What are five good qualities of yours you could name?"

Mark: "Well, I'm reliable, I'm highly skilled, I'm a team player, I have good learning skills and good leadership skills . . ."

Susan: "Okay, now please name . . . let's say three your worst qualities?"

Mark: "Well, I wake up early, not many people like it."

Susan: "Yes, I'm an owl."

Mark: "Yes. I also snore."

*Susan: "Oh" *laughs**

*Mark: *laughs**

Susan: "Well, the test you did at home also seems done well, so congratulations, welcome aboard!"

This specialist is rather naïve of course, yet the root of all evil lies in her offering Mark to fill the blanks rather than establishing personal contact and then analyzing him quickly, actively, and effectively. Let's see how Megan does the job.

Megan: "Hello, Mark."

Mark: "Hello."

Megan: "I can see you're an open-minded person, yet sometimes you feel locked up . . . like maybe now? Is this so?"

Mark: "Yes . . . I . . . well . . ."

Megan: "It's your pose. Your ankles are crossed, and I can see you're looking towards the door

*already, well, don't be afraid, I won't bite." *laughs*
"It's fine, I see you did the test quite well!"*

*Mark: "Okay" *laughs and changes pose* "Yes, I . .
."*

Megan: "Was it hard, the test?"

*Mark: "Well, it was kinda hard . . . but not too much.
I think it was fine."*

Megan: "It was fine? What did you like the most?"

*Mark: "Well, the way, you know, the task was given,
it was very well put . . ."*

*Megan: "Mark, you didn't do the test, did you?
Someone else did it for you?"*

Mark: "Why, no, I . . ."

*Megan: "But you hold yourself well under pressure.
And this is a good quality."*

*Mark: *takes a long pause, then exhales* "Thank
you."*

*Megan: "I cannot recommend you as a senior
specialist as of now, however, I can see you're
motivated and confident. Care to try and complete a*

new test here in the office, in a separate room, right now?"

Mark: *stammers* "I . . ."

Megan: "A junior test perhaps?"

Mark: "Yes please."

Megan: "Perfect."

The difference, as you can see, is tremendous. While Susan merely questions her subject, ticking boxes off one after another, Megan is actively involved. She opens with a Barnum statement, which ends with the claim Mark feels "locked up", guarded from her . . . and she sees confirmation, quickly examining him during a short pause, no more than a glance. She sees a sign of confirmation in his locked-up posture and his new pattern of uncertain behavior, and yet his discomfort must be eased, so Megan quickly moves on to the successfully completed test.

Yet Mark doesn't act as expected, he is not relieved – he looks even more uncomfortable after the test was mentioned! This is a red flag, unpredictability of behavior.

Megan takes a step back, she asks a compassionate question – was the test hard? Mark answers with a generalized (Barnum) statement which could be applied to any test there is, not just the one he supposedly completed at home. Megan is an expert in generalized statements, and she notices it instantly. Mark is trying to *mirror* her behavior – he seeks to re-establish the lost confidence and enters this scanning mode of sorts, something we human beings often do without even realizing it, acting like the person we're talking to, copying their act in order for them to see: *I'm a friend!* And yet their instinctive part, their monkey, is watching quietly: how would this person in front of me react to themselves, what do they have to tell us about themselves, literally?

Megan recognizes not only the Barnum statement, but also the unconscious attempt of Mark's in mirroring her. She reflects it by mirroring back, echoing: "It was fine?" Mirroring back a mirrored behavior is often disorienting, because it carries a strong emotional backlash, which Megan amplifies even more by zooming in: "What did you like *the most?*"

Now Mark is obviously lying. His tone has changed, slowed down: the reason kicked in, putting a muffler on his emotions. Mark speaks slowly, picking words, *inventing* things. Megan no longer has any doubts he didn't do the test.

She asks about it directly, to put this crucial matter to rest straight off. Mark says "no", yet his intonation doesn't change, so he is technically just stalling. By now he understands his lies don't work. He is confused and likely ashamed.

Megan quickly fixes him up by admiring his confidence under stress. Mark didn't show any confidence, and this compliment has nothing to do with reality, yet confirmation bias makes Mark agree. By *agreeing* he feels confident, he accepts Megan's reality and *becomes* confident, or at least much more composed than he just was. This effect is normally called *power of suggestion,* and this is a good tool of active analysis and the emotional management of your subject.

Megan openly offers Mark to redeem himself, prove his own technical knowledge. Mark seems to agree to take the test, yet he stammers. There could be only one reason, and Megan names it: his technical skill is not enough. Instead of discouraging him from the test and discarding him, Megan decides to try and hire Mark as a junior specialist.

So, remember the active analysis sequence well: opening with a generalized (Barnum) statement to break the ice, then zoom in on the most obvious positive characteristic of your subject, counterweighted by cold reading and/or mirroring.

Cold reading means educated guesswork. A lot can be told about your subject from their looks, their dress, their non-verbal signals and tone, their vocabulary. Take everything relevant into account, notice every change that happens, dampen the strike with a positive statement, zoom in on important questions, and so on. If your subject seems to slow down, remember it's their reasonable personality, a less predictable and less primal one kicked in. They could be lying (they could lie on instinct as well, if the lie was prepackaged!)

Mirroring is tricky, and conscious employment of it, same as detection of the attempts of people to mirror you, takes practice. Think of it like a sonar/emitter of sorts, an intuitive device normally more developed in females than males. You take in some emotion from your subject, some impression. Transmit it back by *pretending you're them,* then analyze their response. If you want, you could specifically make them *describe you as you pose as them,* to tell you their opinion of their own character worn as a mask and presented back to them.

If you detect conscious attempts to mirror you, mimic you – the chances are the person you're communicating with belongs to the so-called dark triad: a narcissist, a sociopath, or a Machiavellian (manipulative) type. These types of people use mirroring and cognitive empathy to charm you and pretend to be a very similar, very close person to you in a way you will not be able to comprehend, in a magnetic, hypnotizing way. This bond will grant them emotional control over you, since in fact such people are not necessarily close to you in any way at all. They will often remain very cold, well-controlled, and logical, and yet you will be unable to predict their behavior. Given enough practice when looking for these features, you will be able to spot the dark triad types in conversation and take precautions against their techniques by employing your own (mirroring back).

In the next chapter, we will review the ways to employ the knowledge you obtain during analysis, and we will review both legitimate and criminal employment of analytical techniques and tricks of persuasion, to arm you against possible dark triad types or merely con artists working the same old tricks.

Because a true analyst always stays in control, as objective as possible, and must never be led astray.

19. Persuasion Basics (and Wrongs)

From ancient ages people of certain professions – merchants, diplomats, explorers – were famously employing various tricks of negotiations and persuasion. Persuasion earned money, persuasion saved lives . . . and it destroyed lives. Without persuasion, the whole religions, ideologies, and crucial historical events would simply never happen.

Or, at least it could ruin someone's payday, and this palm reading woman in the street who seemed so concerned and so knowing about Susan, telling her things about her just by the lines on her hand . . . this woman somehow managed to steal Susan's wallet, and it's like a black hole instead of the memories of their meeting in Susan's head. Was the street palmistry woman truly a magician?

So such a thing won't happen to you, we will tell you about how the street palmistry woman does it, for this is her secret criminal profession, a street hypnotist, a con.

We'll also review the work of a "telepathic" medium that makes his living performing with similar techniques onstage, and a complex business deal a certain business lady skilled in analysis and communication has to close despite multiple problems of technical and interpersonal kind.

Let's start with Susan's favorite TV Show, depicting Frank, who is a professional actor and entertainer, stage hypnotist pretending to have telepathic powers. Frank stands before the audience and says:

"They say nothing in the universe happens by accident, and it's impossible to choose someone at random. So now I will choose one of you, a volunteer, following the telepathic signal I receive from the Universe! You! Yes, you, sir!"

At this moment, the trained eyes of Frank scan the faces in the crowd and pick the first mark, a family man in his thirties, balding, seemingly shy. On hearing Frank, the man looks up, then smiles.

"What's there in your breast pocket?" Frank asks him with no pause.

"What?" The man is lost.

"There." Frank points at his breast pocket, yet the man doesn't seem to understand. This can only mean that Frank made a mistake. He expected a man would pull out a personal item, but it seems his breast pocket is empty in the end. Frank makes an impatient face.

"There, there," he repeats in quick succession, and then stops himself. "Oh, doesn't matter, thank you,

we'll ask someone else, I can see my voice already put you in a trance!"

The crowd laughs, the man sits down, and the slip is averted.

Frank points next: "You! Yes, you, sir! What's there in your trouser pocket?"

Frank doesn't actually see the man's trouser pocket. He doesn't have to see it though, as Frank now is working with statistical numbers, not with the observed evidence. The men he picks from the crowd are highly likely to carry something in the pockets he names.

The second man he named gets up and pulls out a wallet and a keyring. Frank keeps gesturing towards the wallet, motioning the man to open it. It's an automatic gesture, a part of Frank's usual routine: if his mark pulls out a container of any kind, he motions for the container to be opened and its contents are shown. This non-verbal command of his is so well-practiced and streamlined his mark opens the wallet automatically, picks up an item, and brings it up to the cameras and the audience, so Frank can see it on the big monitor up close. It's a picture of a 3-year-old girl holding a shabby plush bunny, likely the favorite toy, judging by its condition. The girl has to be the man's daughter, still, there's a certain risk she's not. This is why Frank goes for an inclusive Barnum-shaped statement which seems intimate yet fits any little girl related to this man.

"Yes, it's you, sir! You see, I just received a telepathic message meant for you, it seems . . . it's from your little – what's her name? Jenny! Yes, your little Jenny!" Frank says. The man merely mouthed the name for him to see, yet this could have been seen only by a few faces in the crowd. Frank's pose suggests he already started receiving the telepathic

message – his eyes seem closed, his index fingers are pressed to the temples. Frank speaks into the mouthpiece in a relaxed deep voice. "She tells me to please tell you she might have left her poor . . . poor friend in the car!"'

The man didn't mouth the name of the toy, so Frank had to use a generalized statement. He quickly notices the man thought of the correct item when he heard the word "friend". Yes, it's likely his daughter, she goes everywhere with her favorite bunny toy. And so the man's amused and surprised face fills the big screen behind Frank, the audience watching the man as he is hearing Frank's words, and the look of understanding and revelation on his face is proof enough: the crowd gasps in awe at Frank's supernatural powers, and bursts into applause.

"Please come onstage," Frank invites the man, then gives him the microphone. "So your name is . . .?"

" . . .Alfred!" The man says.

"And this was your . . ."

"This is my daughter Jenny, and yes, she has this toy . . ."

"Her 'friend'?"

"Yes, a bunny by the name Thumper, and . . ."

"You . . .?" Frank gently nudges his mark towards the choices needed for the act.

"Yes, I probably left it in my car you know . . . but how did you know? About Emily, and how could you know I have a car?"

The man asks this despite the fact that in his hands, he is still holding his wallet and the keyring, with a big car alarm fab visible.

The ovation drowns out Frank's words, so the snowman merely gives the camera a smile.

Frank didn't do anything supernatural. He hardly used his attention at all, mostly trusting his trained stage reflexes. The crowd bursts into applause, and yet Frank's work had only just begun: while his audience is content, it's Frank's chance to study his mark better, and prepare his next grand revelation. The man is already impressed, and now, being in the spotlight, he's likely to submit to Frank's will and publically agree with everything Frank says about him or asks from him.

Susan loves Frank's TV show, yet it doesn't help her to understand how persuasion works, how obtained personal informational is employed on practice. Even worse, Susan's belief in supernatural makes magic possible in her world – the mundane tricks other people could find even banal will often seem like something transcending the laws of nature to Susan, making her susceptible to con artists of any kind.

During lunch, walking through a park next to her office, Susan runs into a woman wearing stark ethnical clothes, yet looking motherly and trustworthy. The woman bumps into her seemingly by accident, while Susan is distracted.

"Oh," Susan says, looking at the woman in surprise. "Oh, sorry, I . . ."

"Is the market this way, good lady?" The woman says.

"Y-yes," Susan replies. "Well, it's better to take a subway to . . ."

"Thank you so much!" The woman takes her hand. Susan wants to take it away but wavers – what if it's considered a major sign of disrespect in this exotic lady's traditions?

"Want to thank you, read your fortune on your hand, for free?" The woman suggests with a friendly smile.

Susan smiles back: "Okay."

The woman's tone and posture change radically as she steps up and turns to be faced in the same direction as Susan instead of opposing her. She grasps Susan's hand in a firm professional grip, like a masseur. She flips Susan's hand over and starts muttering to her, deep, without even tracing any lines:

"I know, my daughter, you have this secret passion deep inside, it burns you every day, you want it, but it's fickle and it avoids you, because there's a bad spell put on you by someone close to you."

Susan's head goes around, yet she takes hold of herself. She heard of some people being conned by such palm readers. They say these people can even steal all your money. And Susan has three hundred dollars cash in her wallet. She'd better keep her guard up.

"Look, I don't have any secret passion," she tells the woman, trying to take her hand away, but the woman is holding on to her. Susan says: "You got it wrong. I'm happily married, I have two kids--"

"At work," the woman replies momentarily. "This is about your work."

"Oh," Susan reconsiders what she just heard. A secret passion. Yes, she does want a coordinator's position, and then there's Megan. Susan says: "Yes. I do have this friend back in the office. We . . . compete for a position . . ."

"She cursed you," the woman says, looking straight into Susan's eyes without blinking. Then, as she sees Susan admits such a possibility, the woman steps in, probing her hand like a doctor who just found a very bad disease in her patient. "Yes . . . she probably took something of yours, maybe you

lost something recently, a hairbrush, a lipstick maybe, around your office?"

"Well, in fact I did, just the other week I lost a lipstick," Susan confirms, and then stops. How could this woman know? And Megan, she does seem a little witchy at times, she has green eyes and all. And Frank she saw on TV also warned the audience about some kind of toxic vampiric people who basically look at you wrong, and they set you up for wrong things.

Susan cannot help but remember how many wrongs happened to her in the last two months. She's distracted and disappointed. Megan, how could she do something like this to her?

"There is a cure, don't you worry," the woman tells her in a deep, warm, and sweet voice, like Susan is her little sick daughter. "We can make her curse go away!"

"We can?" Susan asks.

"You have a small coin?" The woman asks.

Automatically, Susan reaches into her purse with her clumsy left hand, the one that the palmistry woman left free. Then her right hand is finally also free, although it does feel limp after it was compressed so.

With her limp right hand, Susan slowly opens her wallet, unzips its small change compartment, and produces a fifty-cent coin.

She never thinks about the fact the wallet is left open in her left hand, as she only opened its small change compartment, and the cash is still locked in. The wallet remains in her field of vision at all times; Susan attention is concentrated on her money, and one small coin? Why not! Here are fifty cents,

Susan can spare as much. Let this woman do to the coin whatever the woman likes.

The palmistry woman makes Susan make a fist around her fifty cents. The woman grabs Susan's fist with the both of her hands and squeezes it with force, clamping Susan's hand down on the hard coin.

The woman quickly mutters an exotic spell, something in a foreign language that sounds mysterious and mind-blowing to Susan, who, like a kid on a carnival, waits for the coin to disappear.

Instead, the woman says:

"Quick, we need a small bill to wrap it in! The curse is inside that coin now! HOLD ON TO IT! HOLD ON TO IT! Don't let the curse escape again!"

She squeezes Susan's right fist very hard, making her hand cramp, and then lets go.

"Quickly, pull out a small bill! And hold to the coin, keep holding! The curse is inside the coin!" The woman's hoarse voice commands. "Need to wrap the coin in a dollar bill! Wrap the coin, quick, or bad things happen!"

Susan tries to pull out a one dollar bill while holding the coin, which now seems to burn her with its malicious curse. It's hard, but she's in control. She doesn't notice the wallet's cash compartment is now also open.

"Now wrap the coin with the small bill! Wrap the coin!" The woman quickly helps Susan make a small origami piece of the bill with the coin wrapped inside. She presses it into Susan's hand.

"Now throw the coin behind you and don't look! Throw it!" The woman commands, and Susan tosses the bill with the coin inside without thinking, and this is when a deep feeling of regret strikes her.

What is she doing now? She just let go of a dollar and fifty cents, just like that! This woman fooled her!

Susan spins back, hoping to retrieve her dollar bill before it's gone. Then she stops and turns back around.

Her wallet is in her left hand, carefully relieved of the three hundred dollars cash. Susan tries to pull out her phone with her right hand and call the police, yet her right hand is too cramped and numb even to unlock the phone, not to mention call a number. Susan is lost. It's like she's just been to some other dimension. There's no sign of the woman around. Did she even exist? What did just happen? She cannot evaluate it. It was supernatural. She was hypnotized. Mind-controlled. Put under.

As feelings return to her hand and she can finally call, Susan realizes she can hardly remember the woman at all. She only remembers her bright exotic clothes. There's nothing coherent she could tell the police.

Susan has got to move on, much poorer yet none wiser.

Back at work, Megan is waiting for her: they have to run a very important 2-hour presentation for the stakeholders of their current project, rebranding of a large pizzeria chain. First Susan must deliver an opening speech, then Megan will present the market research, then the stakeholders must review the history of the brand, the past solutions and their effectiveness, after which Susan and Megan will both present the new proposed solution, and then it's on to snacks, drinks, and the networking.

Susan tells Megan she cannot deliver the fifteen-minute speech in the beginning, she is distressed by an accident with the palm reading woman. Megan turns to their system administrator busy with the projector.

Megan: "Steve, will it be possible to start my part ten minutes earlier? I can deliver the opening speech, but I don't have the whole fifteen minutes of material, I will only take about five, ten minutes at best."

Steven: "That's a problem."

Megan: "Why?"

Steven: "Well, because it TURNS OUT our conference room laptop DIED, and I ONLY found out about it this MORNING when I tried to switch it on. Someone must have spilled WATER on it, and told NO ONE. I brought my OWN laptop, but it's a MAC, and it turns out we don't have the proper connector, SO."

Megan: "Will we be able to start in fifteen minutes as planned?"

Steven: "There's a chance, but I cannot say yet. I'll try to make the connector we need out of two or three other connectors, but it may HAPPEN it just won't WORK. Then I'll have to go out and buy it, which will take about an hour."

Megan: "An hour!"

Steven: "What can I DO, Meg? It's an EMERGENCY. We couldn't KNOW it will happen, so I'm not prepared to deal with it in MINUTES."

Megan: "We cannot cancel this meeting. It may bury the whole project."

Steven: "Not MY problem."

Megan's next impulse is to strike back and reprimand Steve in front of everyone present. How is it not his problem? The reputation of their company is at stake. She could say a lot about Steven's attitude right now.

Megan is a well-trained businesswoman though. She programmed herself to react to every impulse of aggression, which she perceives as red fog descending on her, with mental freeze, followed by a gradual, cold, and restrained analysis of the situation.

If she starts a scene now, she won't make things any better. She only could have made them worse, much worse, throwing accusations around in front of every stakeholder of her project. Right now, as never before, they all must be as strong as they can in terms of teamwork and connection. She hates Steve merely because he informed her of a problem, attacking the messenger. This was *something he didn't cause and couldn't have prevented. He is also extremely upset by what happened, which shows. It must be because he will have to spend half a monthly budget of his department just to replace the dead laptop in their conference room. Her current issue is indeed hers to solve, not his. He was right. She was wrong. After employing common sense and reviewing the situation slowly, Megan is able to dismantle and dissipate a negative emotion threatening not only her current situation, but her entire career – who knows what would happen if she let go and started screaming at Steve, the way she felt like doing at first?*

"You're right," she tells Steven. He is surprised yet happy to hear it. Their team connection was just cemented by her, not destroyed and then rationalized somehow by her reason, late to the party as it ever is, explaining her actions to her in retrospective: "I was angry, and he shouldn't have

crossed me. He said it wasn't his problem, how the hell wasn't it his problem?"

Megan made the right choice, more beneficial to her. Knowing her own personality, she was wise to put such a "mental firewall" between her aggression and the blood sacrifices it demands.

Now she could make a ten-minute opening speech, and then show her slides and diagrams . . . soon her intuition tells her of another problem. She pulls out her portable hard drive.

"Will this thing work with your Mac laptop?" She asks Steven. He gives the hard drive a brief glance, then shakes his head. It won't. She won't be able to run their market research presentation, either.

"Could you just go buy a new PC laptop, straight off, without wasting time with these connectors?" She asks.

"Well, if I leave NOW, won't be back for the next hour and a half," Steven says. "It takes at least THIS long to sign the warranty forms and fill in all the other paperwork."

Megan has to solve this problem. They do fit within their conference room reservation time; they'll have the room for three more hours, because Megan was supposed to arrange snacks and drinks afterward, so the stakeholders would have a chance to network. Susan has the budget for the snacks, so perhaps Megan could serve them upfront, stall the stakeholders, and save the day?

"Suze, we need to open our event with the buffet hour," she whispers to Susan. "You have those three hundred bucks on you?"

Susan pales. She mutters something about how someone just stole the money from her, in a park during their lunch break. Megan can hardly understand the details, but she does realize their snack money is gone. Susan and she must be really down on their luck today.

Megan's impulse is to despair, call the event off, and perhaps lose the client. What could she do? There's nothing that could be done now. Their presentation was doomed from the start. She may as well accept it, submit to the outrageous fortune.

Yet her alarm goes off again. Go cold and restrained. Use common sense. Nothing can be done? No way to save them? Here's the client in front of her, who owns a pizzeria chain. What're three hundred bucks to him?

She approaches the client and smiles at him.

"Excuse me, Mr. Smith, may I ask something? Thank you."

Megan steps closer, draws her client's attention to herself, and speaks fast, in a tone of a conspiring friend:

"I just had this idea: why don't we open with a buffet hour instead of closing with it? And more, we could use this opportunity to introduce them to your product, make them try your wonderful pizzas before they get to decide on their future, right? What do you say?"

"Well . . ." Mr. Smith looks pleased. "I think this is a good idea."

"How fast could you get us your delivery van here?" Her client looks concerned.

"Is ten minutes fine with you?" He asks. "I wish you told me earlier. I'd make a call right now."

"Please!" Megan smiles at him again. "I'll entertain our guests in the meantime."

Ten minutes is perfectly fine, as she needs as much for her opening speech. Then they're going to have a nice pizza party, while Steven replaces the conference room laptop. Their presentation is saved.

This is a happy ending even for Susan, who lost nothing in the end, as their snacks and drinks were sponsored by the client, who didn't mind at all.

Still, Susan is none wiser, while Megan developed a new business strategy.

This is about the only way to show to you how persuasion works, and how an active, a proactive analyst may not only work with their subjects to obtain personal knowledge about them, but also establish positive communication with them, which ends in strengthening social and business connections for common benefit of everyone involved, a mindful act with no casualties and no burnt bridges.

20. Afterword

We will not lie to you and pretend there is some kind of social justice, or universal justice, ruling over this Earth. The world we live in is unfair, and it's easy to succeed in life being a dishonest, treacherous, Machiavellian type of person, for whom their personal gain justifies any sort of means.

These people exist. They do succeed. They become major power figures and rule the world. They change the way our planet works, they start wars and establish religions. They kill or rob millions of people in the process. They die rich, happy, and successful, in their beds, one hundred and something years old. This is how it was before, and this is how it is now, and we cannot be blind to the facts of it.

This doesn't mean however that this is how it should be. If only honest people, kind and mindful people, who care about what happens to the humankind as a whole, who sincerely wish everyone around them nothing but the best – if only these people were as well versed in analysis and persuasion as the dishonest and selfish types!

The problem is honesty is an artificial construct. Full objectivity hardly exists when we talk about human character. We often lie for good causes, and never worry about us doing something bad by doing so. We easily circumvent and override our conscience when we need to. To many of us, deep inside, social norms and morals hardly mean anything at all – only the *peer pressure* matters to us, the fact that, *if people around us knew,* they'd shun us and hate us, or even lock us up for our actions.

But if no one will ever know, is there really anything that stops us? Anything our reason will not be able to dismantle, neutralize, rationalize and make go away? It only takes a desire strong enough to overrule the will, or catch us unawares, we will temporarily aligned with our primal needs, our common sense left out as it happens.

This is why, instead of conscience, we appeal to your honor.

The modern culture is much more peaceful, more reasonable than it used to be. We – or at least the most of us – no longer think in terms of sin and virtue. We do not deprive ourselves of pleasures for ritualistic, spiritual reasons; at least we no longer do it with fervor and zeal that could once destroy a family or consume a life. We accept our basic desires – catering to one's flesh, seeking the life of luxury is no longer morally questionable or detestable in our world.

Every medal has two sides however. The present human society, speaking equally of the Western and the Eastern society, seems to value ego above everything else; "being oneself", "being special", "staying true to one's inner nature", and "listening to one's heart" becoming the staples of the quest for happiness, which is the ultimate goal of our universal culture. We fail to notice this, but in the present times, we seem to serve a golden calf of our 'self-esteem' and 'self-worth' with the zeal we used to reserve for witch burnings, and we suffer, and make other people suffer, seeking an unobtainable state called "high enough self-esteem".

This is because the true key to personal happiness doesn't lie in catering to the primal urges, same as it doesn't lie in disabling or suppressing them, as many religions tend to claim. The happiness hides in balance between the desires of the flesh and those of the mind, our reason – the chatty computer – being employed as a tool to seek solutions to the problems plaguing our monkey, and not vice versa.

Too many people live their life on instinct alone, repeating a simple routine and compensating for the lack of free will with "spiritual" introspection, which yields them nothing except for occasional bouts of grandiose sense of self-worth. Too many people use their reason to explain their actions to themselves *after* they act, without employing common sense beforehand at all. Their couch potato of a brain is watching their life in retrospective, after it's already happened, and tells them why it all had to be so.

The main goal of this book is to teach you to do otherwise. Observe, analyze, and then act. Satisfy your mind, and then cater to your body. Switch on the computer and click its mental keys a bit before the monkey decides what to do.

And this is when you will understand our life doesn't have to be a rat race, a Darwinian battle of primates for status, for food and shelter, for the praise of opposite sex (or the same sex). Instead, we could be attentive, helpful, and mindful towards each other, connect and grow strong instead of falling divided. None of us has to be lonely, shunned by others for an unknown reason, and ashamed of themselves. Our common sense always prevails in the end . . . the problem is it often prevails when it's too late.

And this is about the only thing that stands between us, human beings, and our personal happiness, which then adds up to our common good.

We will be happy if this book brings you one step closer to this vision.

21. Disclaimer

The information contained in **"Dark Psychology Secrets & The Art Of Reading People -2 in 1-"** and its components, is meant to serve as a comprehensive collection of strategies that the author of this eBook has done research about. Summaries, strategies, tips and tricks are only recommendations by the author, and reading this eBook will not guarantee that one's results will exactly mirror the author's results.

The author of this Ebook has made all reasonable efforts to provide current and accurate information for the readers of this eBook. The author and its associates will not be held liable for any unintentional errors or omissions that may be found.

The material in the Ebook may include information by third parties. Third party materials comprise of opinions expressed by their owners. As such, the author of this eBook does not assume responsibility or liability for any third party material or opinions.

The publication of third party material does not constitute the author's guarantee of any information, products, services, or opinions contained within third party material. Use of third party material does not guarantee that your results will mirror our results. Publication of such third party material is simply a recommendation and expression of the author's own opinion of that material.

Whether because of the progression of the Internet, or the unforeseen changes in company policy and editorial submission guidelines, what is stated as fact at the time of this writing may become outdated or inapplicable later.

this Ebook whole or in parts. No parts of this report may be reproduced or retransmitted in any forms whatsoever without the written expressed and signed permission from the author.

This self-help book is very experimental in nature. We never bothered you with references to other books and studies so far, because we didn't want to distract you from the reading. Below you will find the list of recommended reads related to people analysis, and the psychology and neurophysiology involved.

22. Recommended Reading

Erich Fromm "The Art of Listening"

Erich Fromm "Escape from Freedom" ("The Fear of Freedom")

Daniel Kahneman "Thinking, Fast and Slow"

David Rock "Your Brain at Work"

Eric Berne "Games People Play: The Psychology of Human Relationships"

Tania Singer "Caring Economics: Conversations on Altruism and Compassion, Between Scientists, Economists, and the Dalai Lama"

Konstantin Stanislawski "Method of Physical Action"

Andrew Bradbury "Develop Your NLP Skills"

Christian Keysers "The Empathic Brain", "Mirror Neurons"

9 781793 244451